First World War
and Army of Occupation
War Diary
France, Belgium and Germany

51 DIVISION
154 Infantry Brigade
Royal Scots (Lothian Regiment)
9th Battalion
1 January 1916 - 31 January 1918

WO95/2887/5

The Naval & Military Press Ltd
www.nmarchive.com
Published in association with The National Archives

Published by

The Naval & Military Press Ltd

Unit 10 Ridgewood Industrial Park,

Uckfield, East Sussex,

TN22 5QE England

Tel: +44 (0) 1825 749494

www.naval-military-press.com

www.nmarchive.com

This diary has been reprinted in facsimile from the original. Any imperfections are inevitably reproduced and the quality may fall short of modern type and cartographic standards.

Contents

War Diary	Bivouacs Meaulte	01/08/1916	01/08/1916
War Diary	Mametz Wood	02/08/1916	06/08/1916
War Diary	Bivouacs Near Dernancourt	06/08/1916	09/08/1916
War Diary	Erondelle	09/08/1916	11/08/1916
War Diary	Ebblinghem	11/08/1916	14/08/1916
War Diary	Armentieres	14/08/1916	15/08/1916
War Diary	Trenches	15/08/1916	16/08/1916
War Diary	Armentieres Trenches	17/08/1916	21/08/1916
War Diary	Armentieres Billets	22/08/1916	25/08/1916
War Diary	Camp Near Bailleul	26/08/1916	31/08/1916
Heading	War Diary 9th Battalion (Highlanders) The Royal Scots From 1st Sept 1916 To 30th Sept 1916 Vol 19		
War Diary	Training Camp 1 Mile S.E. Of Bailleul	01/09/1916	02/09/1916
War Diary	Nieppe	02/09/1916	03/09/1916
War Diary	Trenches North Of River Lys.	03/09/1916	08/09/1916
War Diary	Armentiers Trenches (Houplines)	09/09/1916	15/09/1916
War Diary	Houplines (Trenches)	15/09/1916	22/09/1916
War Diary	Erquinghem Billets	23/09/1916	24/09/1916
War Diary	Estaires Billets	25/09/1916	30/09/1916
Heading	War Diary 9th Batt. (Highrs) The Royal Scots From 1st Oct To 31st Oct		
War Diary	Candas Billets	01/10/1916	02/10/1916
War Diary	Famechon Billets	03/10/1916	03/10/1916
War Diary	Bus-Les-Artois Billets	04/10/1916	07/10/1916
War Diary	Colincamps Bivouacs	08/10/1916	12/10/1916
War Diary	Billets Louvencourt	12/10/1916	16/10/1916
War Diary	Forcevillers (Camp)	17/10/1916	17/10/1916
War Diary	Lealvillers Billets	18/10/1916	21/10/1916
War Diary	Milly-Maillet Bivouacs	22/10/1916	25/10/1916
War Diary	Trenches In Front Of Auchonvillers	26/10/1916	26/10/1916
War Diary	Trenches East Of Auchonvillers	27/10/1916	30/10/1916
War Diary	Lealvillers Billets	31/10/1916	31/10/1916
Heading	War Diary 9th Battalion (Highlanders) The Royal Scots From 1st November 1916 To 30th November 1916		
War Diary	Lealvillers Billets	01/11/1916	04/11/1916
War Diary	Mailly Wood Bivouacs	05/11/1916	07/11/1916
War Diary	Trenches East Of Auchonvillers	08/11/1916	12/11/1916
War Diary	Mailly Wood Camp	13/11/1916	13/11/1916
War Diary	Operations At Beaumont Hamel	13/11/1916	19/11/1916
War Diary	Camp Mailly Wood	20/11/1916	22/11/1916
War Diary	Camp Hedauville	23/11/1916	23/11/1916
War Diary	Puchevillers Billets	24/11/1916	25/11/1916
War Diary	Aveluy Huts	26/11/1916	27/11/1916
War Diary	Ovillers Huts	28/11/1916	30/11/1916
Heading	War Diary 9th Batt (Highrs) The Royal Scots From 1/12/16 To 31/12/16		
War Diary	Ovillers Huts	01/12/1916	02/12/1916
War Diary	Dugouts W Of Courcelette	03/12/1916	05/12/1916
War Diary	Trenches	06/12/1916	08/12/1916
War Diary	Ovillers Huts	09/12/1916	09/12/1916
War Diary	Billets Bouzincourt	10/12/1916	10/12/1916
War Diary	Billets	11/12/1916	11/12/1916
War Diary	Bouzincourt	11/12/1916	15/12/1916
War Diary	Bruce Huts Aveluy	16/12/1916	20/12/1916
War Diary	Wolfe Huts Ovillers	21/12/1916	23/12/1916
War Diary	Trenches	24/12/1916	26/12/1916

War Diary	Ovillers Huts	27/12/1916	27/12/1916
War Diary	Bouzincourt	28/12/1916	31/12/1916
Heading	War Diary 9th Battalion (Highlanders) The Royal Scots From 1st January 1917 To 31st January 1917		
War Diary	Bouzincourt	01/01/1917	02/01/1917
War Diary	Ovillers Huts	03/01/1917	07/01/1917
War Diary	Trenches	08/01/1917	09/01/1917
War Diary	Wolfe Huts	10/01/1917	12/01/1917
War Diary	Val De Maison	13/01/1917	13/01/1917
War Diary	Fienvillers	14/01/1917	14/01/1917
War Diary	Oneux	15/01/1917	15/01/1917
War Diary	Morlay	16/01/1917	31/01/1917
Heading	War Diary February 1917 1/9th Bn The Royal Scots (Hrs)		
War Diary	Morlay	01/02/1917	04/02/1917
War Diary	Lamotte-Buleux	05/02/1917	05/02/1917
War Diary	Marche-Ville	06/02/1917	06/02/1917
War Diary	Buire-Au-Bois	07/02/1917	07/02/1917
War Diary	Blangerval	08/02/1917	08/02/1917
War Diary	Bailleul	09/02/1917	10/02/1917
War Diary	Ecoivres Huts	11/02/1917	26/02/1917
War Diary	Trenches	27/02/1917	04/03/1917
War Diary	Maroueil	05/03/1917	10/03/1917
War Diary	Bois De Maroeuil	11/03/1917	15/03/1917
War Diary	Frevillers	16/03/1917	21/03/1917
War Diary	Maroeuil Huts	22/03/1917	22/03/1917
War Diary	Ecurie	23/03/1917	31/03/1917
Heading	War Diary 9th Batt (Hrs) The Royal Scots From 1st April 1917 To 30th April		
War Diary	Ecurie	01/04/1917	02/04/1917
War Diary	Maroeuil Huts	03/04/1917	06/04/1917
War Diary	Trenches	07/04/1917	11/04/1917
War Diary	Y Huts Laresset	12/04/1917	12/04/1917
War Diary	Laresset	12/04/1917	14/04/1917
War Diary	Line	15/04/1917	25/04/1917
War Diary	Averdoingt	26/04/1917	30/04/1917
Map	Map		
Map	Sketch C		
Map	Sketch D		
Operation(al) Order(s)	Operation Order No. 70	05/04/1917	05/04/1917
Miscellaneous	Reference Operation Order No. 70	05/04/1917	05/04/1917
Miscellaneous	Amendment To Operation Order No. 70	06/04/1917	06/04/1917
Miscellaneous	Amendment To O.O.70	07/04/1917	07/04/1917
Map	Trench Map		
Miscellaneous	O.O 78 G	22/04/1917	22/04/1917
Miscellaneous	Instructions For Offensive No.1	21/04/1917	21/04/1917
Heading	War Diary 9th Batt. (Hrs) The Royal Scots From 1st May 1917 To 31st May		
Heading	Cover For Documents. Nature Of Enclosures. War		
War Diary	Averdoingt	01/05/1917	11/05/1917
War Diary	Y Huts Laresset	12/05/1917	13/05/1917
War Diary	Arras	14/05/1917	24/05/1917
War Diary	Line	24/05/1917	31/05/1917
Map	Map		
Heading	War Diary 9th Battalion (Highlanders) The Royal Scots From 1 June 1917 To 30 June 1917		

War Diary	Arras	01/06/1917	01/06/1917
War Diary	Villers-Brulin	02/06/1917	04/06/1917
War Diary	Valhuon	05/06/1917	05/06/1917
War Diary	Lisbourg	06/06/1917	06/06/1917
War Diary	Nordausques	07/06/1917	21/06/1917
War Diary	Wulverdinghe	22/06/1917	30/06/1917
Heading	War Diary 9th Battalion (Highlanders) The Royal Scots From 1st July 1917 To 31st July 1917		
War Diary	Wulverdinghe	01/07/1917	08/07/1917
War Diary	D Camp A 30 Central	09/07/1917	09/07/1917
War Diary	Line	10/07/1917	12/07/1917
War Diary	Houtkerque	13/07/1917	21/07/1917
War Diary	Windmill Camp	22/07/1917	30/07/1917
War Diary	W. Side Canal Bank C.25.a.	31/07/1917	31/07/1917
Heading	War Diary 9th Battn (Hrs) The Royal Scots From 1st August 1917 To 31st August 1917		
War Diary		01/08/1917	11/08/1917
War Diary	Bayenghem	12/08/1917	22/08/1917
War Diary	Tunnelling Camp St Janster Biezen	23/08/1917	28/08/1917
War Diary	Murat Camp	29/08/1917	31/08/1917
Heading	War Diary 9th Battn (Hrs) The Royal Scots From 1st Sept 1917 To 30th Sept 1917 Vol 31		
War Diary	Murat Camp	01/09/1917	03/09/1917
War Diary	Dirty Bucket Camp	04/09/1917	05/09/1917
War Diary	Line	06/09/1917	08/09/1917
War Diary	Canal Bank	09/09/1917	11/09/1917
War Diary	Siege Camp	12/09/1917	18/09/1917
War Diary	Line	19/09/1917	21/09/1917
War Diary	Siege Camp	22/09/1917	23/09/1917
War Diary	Poperinghe	24/09/1917	28/09/1917
War Diary	Courcelles	29/09/1917	30/09/1917
Miscellaneous	Appendix I To Instructions For Offensive Operation I 2	28/09/1917	28/09/1917
Miscellaneous	Instructions For Offensive Operations I 2	17/09/1917	17/09/1917
Heading	War Diary 9th Battalion (Highlanders) The Royal Scots From 1-10-17 To 31-10-17		
War Diary	Courcelles	01/10/1917	04/10/1917
War Diary	Line	05/10/1917	13/10/1917
War Diary	York Lines M.22.b.8.3.	14/10/1917	21/10/1917
War Diary	Line	21/10/1917	28/10/1917
War Diary	Izel-Le-Hameau	29/10/1917	31/10/1917
Map	Trench Map		
Heading	154th Brigade 51st Division 9th Battalion The Royal Scots November 1917		
War Diary	Izel Le Hameau	01/11/1917	17/11/1917
War Diary	Bapaume	18/11/1917	18/11/1917
War Diary	Lechelle	19/11/1917	19/11/1917
War Diary	Metz	20/11/1917	20/11/1917
War Diary	Line	21/11/1917	23/11/1917
War Diary	Metz	24/11/1917	24/11/1917
War Diary	Ville	25/11/1917	30/11/1917
Miscellaneous	Battalion Report On Operations		
Miscellaneous	Headquarters 154th. Infantry Brigade	27/11/1917	27/11/1917
Miscellaneous	Report A Communication		
Miscellaneous	Report On Communications	27/11/1917	27/11/1917
Diagram etc	Line Diagram Of Communications		
Diagram etc	Line Diagram Of Bn Communications		

Miscellaneous			
Miscellaneous	Boundaries		
Miscellaneous	Instructions For Offensive Operations A.1/2	17/11/1917	17/11/1917
Miscellaneous	Appendix I To Instructions For Offensive Operations A.1/2	18/11/1917	18/11/1917
Heading	War Diary For December 1917 Of 9th Royal Scots		
War Diary	Rocquigny	01/12/1917	01/12/1917
War Diary	Bertincourt	01/12/1917	01/12/1917
War Diary	Line	01/12/1917	05/12/1917
War Diary	Fremicourt	05/12/1917	16/12/1917
War Diary	Line	17/12/1917	22/12/1917
War Diary	Fremicourt	23/12/1917	30/12/1917
War Diary	Line	31/12/1917	31/12/1917
Heading	War Diary 9th Battn (Hrs) The Royal Scots From 1st Jan 1918 To 31st Jan 1918		
War Diary	Line	01/01/1918	07/01/1918
War Diary	Fremicourt	08/01/1918	15/01/1918
War Diary	Lebucquiere	15/01/1918	19/01/1918
War Diary	Courcelles Le Comte	21/01/1918	21/01/1918
War Diary	Bailleulval	21/01/1918	31/01/1918
Operation(al) Order(s)	9th Battn (Hrs) The Royal Scot Operation Order No. 141	06/01/1918	06/01/1918
Miscellaneous	Relief Table		
Operation(al) Order(s)	Operation Order No. 143.	14/01/1918	14/01/1918
Miscellaneous	Operation Order No. 143		
Operation(al) Order(s)	Operation Order No. 144.	19/01/1918	19/01/1918

WO95/2887/5

9 Battalion The Royal Scots

9TH BN ROYAL SCOTS

JAN ~~MAR~~ 1916-JAN 1918

From 27 DIV 81 BDE

To 15 DIV 46 BDE

2136

Reference Maps
French Sheet 62. C.N.W.
AMIENS. Sheet 17. 1/100000
French. Sheet 67. 1/40000

WAR DIARY
or
INTELLIGENCE SUMMARY.
(Erase heading not required.)

Army Form C. 2118.

9th Bnl (N9)
R. Reyne Lieut Col

Instructions regarding War Diaries and Intelligence
Summaries are contained in F. S. Regs., Part II.
and the Staff Manual respectively. Title pages
will be prepared in manuscript.

Place	Date	Hour	Summary of Events and Information	Remarks and references to Appendices
VAUX X	1/1/16		B Coy and 1 platoon C Coy relieved D Coy and 1 platoon C Coy at MOULIN DE FARGNY. 2 platoons D Coy proceeded to BATTLE DUGOUTS. 3 platoons C Coy at VAUX WOOD. The went to relieve march arrival.	S.S.
VAUX X	2/1/16		Battalion as on 1st inst.	S.S.
VAUX X	3/1/16		About 1 a.m. 2nd Lt J. R. BLACK and a party of 27 NCos and men proceeded from VAUX and after providing reserves, 2nd Lt BLACK and 8 men bombed German post at LA GRENOUILLIERE, using 33 grenades and during assault Sentient No 7468 Pte. C.Q. TEMPERMAN were wounded but were brought back safely.	S.S.
			D Coy and 1 platoon C Coy relieved B Coy and 1 platoon C Coy at MOULIN DE FARGNY. 2 platoons B Coy proceeded to VAUX and 2 platoons to BATTLE DUGOUTS. 3 platoons C Coy at VAUX WOOD.	
VAUX X	4/1/16		Position of Companies as on 3rd inst.	S.S.
VAUX X	5/1/16		About 3 a.m. Germans surprised D Coy left listening post in T.11 coming near from Béthune captured and CROW'S NEST said J. Snaple Capt of report 9 Bn. (N9).	S.S.

2353 Wt. W254+/1454 700,000 5/15 D. D. & L.   A.D.S.S./Forms/C. 2118.

WAR DIARY
or
INTELLIGENCE SUMMARY.

(Erase heading not required.)

Instructions regarding War Diaries and Intelligence
Summaries are contained in F. S. Regs., Part II.
and the Staff Manual respectively. Title pages
will be prepared in manuscript.

Reference Maps
FRANCE/Sheet 62. C. N.W
AMIENS about 15½/½ 10000
FRANCE
PÉRONNE about 157½ 1/40000

9th N-F (Tp)
The Payne Foto

Place	Date	Hour	Summary of Events and Information	Remarks and references to Appendices
			throwing about 15-20 grenades, wounding No 3103 Pte G. REID and taking Prisoner No 2258 Pte T. E. RUTHERFORD - No 2097 Pte J. M. DALZIEL was also slightly wounded but returns to duty - The garrison of "B" general rifle and machine gun fire and one German is believed to have been hit. 2 officers and 74 other ranks of "A" Coy for instruction in patrol work on the REGT. were attached to "A" Coy for instruction in patrol work on the march. The Scouts patrolled as usual.	J. S.
VAUX	6/1/16 4 p.m.		"B" Coy and 1 platoon "C" Coy relieved "D" Coy and 1 platoon "C" Coy at MOULIN DE FARGNY - 2 platoons "D" Coy relieved 2 platoons of "A" Coy at VAUX and 2 platoons "C" Coy at VAUX WOOD. BATTLE DUGOUTS - 3 platoons "C" Coy at VAUX WOOD. Position of Companies as on 5th. The Scouts patrolled as usual.	J. S.
VAUX	7/1/16		"D" Coy and 1 platoon "C" Coy relieved "B" Coy and 1 platoon "C" Coy at MOULIN DE FARGNY - On relief 2 platoons "B" Coy proceeded to VAUX and 2 platoons to BATTLE DUGOUTS - 3 platoons "C" Coy at VAUX WOOD - The Scouts patrolled as usual -	J. S.
VAUX	9/1/16		Position of Companies as on 7th inst. 3524 Pte T. GRANT and 1017 were wounded.	

V. Trevor Capt. & Adjt
9th N-F (T.F.)

Reference Maps:
PRANCE - Sheet 62 C. N.W.
MAIENT - Sheet 7. F/10000
FRANCE - Sheet 57 D. 1/40000

Army Form C. 2118

WAR DIARY
or
~~INTELLIGENCE SUMMARY~~
(*Erase heading not required.*)

Instructions regarding War Diaries and Intelligence Summaries are contained in F. S. Regs., Part II. and the Staff Manual respectively. Title Pages will be prepared in manuscript.

9th 2/8 (City)
The Royne Part to

III

Place	Date	Hour	Summary of Events and Information	Remarks and references to Appendices
VAUX	9/1/16		in VAUX by rifle bullet. Sentends followed the road as usual	J.J.
			Position of Company as in 7th + 8th. 1255 Cpl J.C. ITEE was wounded in VAUX WOOD by shrapnel. Sentends followed the road as usual.	J.J.
VAUX SUZANNE	10/1/16		The Battalion was relieved by the 18th MANCHESTER REGT. Worship of Nos B Coy and 3 platoons Coy taking place in the morning about 10 o'clock and that of D Coy and 1 platoon Coy after dark about 6 p.m. on relief the Company proceeds to SUZANNE where they spent the night under canvas. 2nd Lt J.R. BLACK and 17 other ranks are left at VAUX to give further in. Ihination to 18th MANCHESTER REGT.	J.J.
SUZANNE ETINEHEM	11/1/16		Between 12.30 P.M. and 2.15 P.M. the Germans shelled SUZANNE with 3840 shells and 7442 Pte W. CALDWELL was killed and 1378 Pte E.A. GRENVILLE died the same day of wounds then received. Lieut R.M. MENZIES and seven other ranks were wounded. One riding horse was killed. At 3 P.M. the Battalion left SUZANNE	J.J.

T. Snowden
Capt + Adjt
9 th Royne Part to

1875. Wt. W593/826 1,000,000 4/15 J.B.C. & A. A.D.S.S./Forms/C. 2118.

Army Form C. 2118

WAR DIARY

or

INTELLIGENCE SUMMARY

~~(Erase heading not required.)~~

Instructions regarding War Diaries and Intelligence Summaries are contained in F. S. Regs., Part II. and the Staff Manual respectively. Title Pages will be prepared in manuscript.

Reference Snappes:
FRANCE Sheet 62 C. N.W
ATH.1ST.— Sheet 17 1/100,000
FRANCE — Sheet 57 D 1/40,000

9 H. By Att'd
The Royal Scots.

IV

Place	Date	Hour	Summary of Events and Information	Remarks and references to Appendices
ETNEHEM	12/1/16		H.Q. and A and B Coys proceeding to ETNEHEM (6 miles) and Coys and D Companies to CAPPILLY (about 8 miles) and were being repeating billetts for the night.—	A.D.J.
BAZIEUX		At 9.30 a.m H.Q. and A and B Coys formed and marched 10 km Coy's A Coys proceeded and marched to BAZIEUX (12 miles) whilst they arriving about 1.30 p.m and 2.30 p.m respectively. Capt R.M. DUDGEON, Adjutant of the Battalion, left the Battalion at ETNEHEM, having been gazetted Major and Temporarily app. pointed Second in Command of the 7/6 th R. WARWICK REG.T	A.D.J.
BAZIEUX	13/1/16		Battalion resting at BAZIEUX.— during this period the Battalion was present training in (1) close order drill (2) Platoon and drill	A.D.J.
	24/1/16		(3) Coy in attack (4) grenade and and (7s) route marches. Special classes of instruction were also conducted in machine gun, improving signalling.— 2nd Lt. J. R. BLACK and 7 men rejoins the Battalion on 13th.— Reinforcement of 3 M.G.O.s and P. E. C. HONEYMAN, 2nd Lt. J. Bruce Capt Adjt. 9 H. By Att'd Scots.	A.D.J.

Army Form C. 2118

WAR DIARY
or
INTELLIGENCE SUMMARY
(*Erase heading not required.*)

Instructions regarding War Diaries and Intelligence Summaries are contained in F. S. Regs., Part II. and the Staff Manual respectively. Title Pages will be prepared in manuscript.

9 #/3h (H.)   The Royal Scots

Place	Date	Hour	Summary of Events and Information	Remarks and references to Appendices
BAIZIEUX	25/1/16		B. E. CORBETT and 2nd Lieut A. F. CAMERON) joined the Battalion on 16th inst from ENGLAND and 1 officer (2nd Lieut W. B. BENTLEY) on 7th inst.	I. D.
BEAUCOURT QUART			The Battalion became III Army Troops in place the 1/6th KING'S LIVERPOOL REGT and removed from BAIZIEUX at 6.30 AM as follows:-	
			H.Q and officers of B Coy and 150 other ranks to BERTRANCOURT (9 miles by march route.	
			Lt. Col A.J. BLAIR. Captn. R.S. LINDSAY and 2 medical Coy and 710 Other ranks to BEAUQUESNE by march bro.	I. D.
			3 officers D Coy and 100 Other ranks to CAMBRIN by march bro.	
			1 officer Coy and 50 other ranks to HAMELICOURT by march bro.	
			2 officers A Coy and 100 Other ranks to TOUTENCOURT (9 miles) by march route	
			2 officers A Coy and 50 Other ranks to PUCHEVILLERS (miles) by march route.	
			and were billetted at these places. Lieut J.G. BURNS and 100 Other ranks left billetted at BAIZIEUX - Lt Col AS BLAIR became Commandant III Army Troops	

J. Brown Capt & Adjt
9th Royal Scots

Army Form C. 2118

WAR DIARY

or

INTELLIGENCE SUMMARY

(Erase heading not required.)

Instructions regarding War Diaries and Intelligence Summaries are contained in F. S. Regs., Part II. and the Staff Manual respectively. Title Pages will be prepared in manuscript.

Place	Date	Hour	Summary of Events and Information	Remarks and references to Appendices
BERTRAN-COURT	26/1/16		Revd. BURNS and Two Men ranks left BATZIEUX at 8.30am and proceeded by motor bus to BEAUQUESNE.	J.J.
BERTRAN-COURT	27/1/16 to 31/1/16		A Detachment engaged in work at their billets under R.E. The work consisted of quarrying, hurdle making, digging trenches, and at BEAUQUESNE the greater number of the men were employed as clerks, orderlies, grooms, cooks and servants. During the period 1/1/16 to 31/1/16 the weather has comparatively dry, with no frost, and mild. The health of the battalion was good and the morale excellent.	J.J.

J. Fraser,
Capt & Adjt,
9th Royal Scots.

1875   Wt. W593/826 1,000,000 4/15 J.B.C. & A. A.D.S.S./Forms/C. 2118.

Third Army.

9th Bn. (Res.)
The Tyne Scots.

Reference map.
FRANCE. Sheet 57 D. 1/40,000

WAR DIARY

or

INTELLIGENCE SUMMARY

(Erase heading not required.)

Army Form C. 2118

Instructions regarding War Diaries and Intelligence Summaries are contained in F. S. Regs., Part II. and the Staff Manual respectively. Title Pages will be prepared in manuscript.

Place	Date	Hour	Summary of Events and Information	Remarks and references to Appendices
BERTRAN- COURT	1/2/16		Detachments engaged in work at their stations.	J.G.
- do -	2/2/16		One officer and 57 other ranks of detachment at TOUTENCOURT and 3 officers and 43 other ranks of Detachment at MONDICOURT proceeded to BERTRANCOURT for work under R.E. there. Remainder of Detachments at these places and the other Detachments carried on work as usual.	J.G.
- do -	3/2/16 to 4/2/16		Detachments carried on work as usual	J.G.
- do -	5/2/16		Detachment at TOUTENCOURT marched to AMPLIER where it should billet for work on hutting under the R.E. Other Detachments as before	J.G.
- do -	6/2/16 to 8/2/16		The usual work was carried on by the Detachments. On 8/2/16 a draft of 27 other ranks joined for duty.	J.G.
- do -	9/2/16		Detachment at PUCHEVILLERS proceeded by march route to AUTHEUILE where it billeted for work on hutting. Other Detachments as before.	J.G.
- do -	10/2/16 11/2/16		Usual work was carried on by Detachments. A draft of 8 other ranks (machine gunners) joined for duty on 11/2/16.	J.G.

J. Snee Captain,
9th Royal Scots.

23

1875 Wt. W593/826 1,000,000 4/15 J.B.|C. & A. A.D.S.S./Forms/C. 2118.

Army Form C. 2118

WAR DIARY

or

INTELLIGENCE SUMMARY

(*Erase heading not required.*)

9th Bn (J.P.)
The Royal Scots

Instructions regarding War Diaries and Intelligence
Summaries are contained in F.S. Regs., Part II.
and the Staff Manual respectively. Title Pages
will be prepared in manuscript.

Place	Date	Hour	Summary of Events and Information	Remarks and references to Appendices
BEAUQUESNE	12/7/16		Detachment at PANNEToN marched to MUNDICOURT and finished etc. work and there for work. HQ marched from BERTRANCOURT to BEAUQUESNE where it billeted. Other detachments as before	J.S.
- do -	13/7/16		Detachments carried on work -	J.S.
- do -	14/7/16		Detachment at CAUSMENT proceeded by motor bus to HENCY where it billeted for work on railway siding. Other detachments as before -	J.S.
- do -	15/7/16 to 23/7/16		Detachments carried on work as usual.	J.S.
- do -	24/7/16		Detachment at AUTHEULE marched to AMPLIER where it billeted for work under R.E. Other detachments continued work as usual	J.S.
- do -	25/7/16 to 29/7/16		Detachments carried on work as usual	J.S.
- do -	29/7/16		Detachment at HENCY joined 51st Division. Procceded to Detachments unknown. Other detachments carried on as usual.	J.S.
			During the period 1/2/16 to 29/7/16 the weather was fairly good but has first towards the end of month. The health of the Battalion has been very good and the moral excellent.
J. Smith Capt & Adjt
9th Royal Scots

1875   Wt. W593/826 1,000,000 4/15   J.B.C. & A.   A.D.S.S./Forms/C. 2118.

Reference maps:-
FRANCE - LENS 11 Hugoo
TRENCH MAP. 57. N.N.W. 1/40000

Army Form C. 2118

WAR DIARY

or

INTELLIGENCE SUMMARY

(Erase heading not required.)

9 ᵗʰ (Bn (H⁹)
The Royal Scots

Instructions regarding War Diaries and Intelligence Summaries are contained in F. S. Regs., Part II. and the Staff Manual respectively. Title Pages will be prepared in manuscript.

1 . 3 . 16 7

Initial Pen 29 2 16 —

Place	Date	Hour	Summary of Events and Information	Remarks and references to Appendices
PIERREGOT	1/3/16		The Battalion ceased to be Army troops and was attached at PIERREGOT and joined the 152ⁿᵈ Infantry Brigade, 51ˢᵗ Division as follows:- The Battalion at MONDICOURT left there at 8.30 a.m and proceeded to AMPLIER where it joined up with the detachment there and left detachments previously located by march route to PIERREGOT (via BEAUVIGNE, PUCHEVILLERS and RUBEMPRE) where they arrived about 5 P.M (Distance about 17 miles) - HQ and detachment at BEAUVIGNE left at 1 P.M and marched to PIERREGOT by the same route where it arrived about 3.15 P.M (distance about 7 miles) and joined the detachment from HEILLY which had arrived at MIRVAUX the previous day. The Battalion billeted at PIERREGOT -	
" "	2.3.16 to 5.3.16		The Battalion remained at PIERREGOT and carried out training - Special classes for Lewis gunners, Snipers, signallers and Grenadiers were started -	
DOULLENS	6.3.16		The Battalion marched at 8.30 a.m and marched with the 7ᵗʰ Brigade to DOULLENS (via RUBEMPRE, PUCHEVILLERS, BEAUVIGNE, TERRAMESNIL) about 12 miles, where billeted -	

J. Fraser Capt for (?)
9 ᵗʰ Royal Scots

1875 Wt. W 593/826 1,000,000 4/15 J.B.C. & A. A.D.S.S./Forms/C. 2118.

Army Form C. 2118

Reference maps
FRANCE: LENS II 1/100,000
TRENCH MAP. 57.B. N.W. I 1/10,000

Instructions regarding War Diaries and Intelligence
Summaries are contained in F. S. Regs., Part II.
and the Staff Manual respectively. Title Pages
will be prepared in manuscript.

WAR DIARY
or
INTELLIGENCE SUMMARY
(Erase heading not required.)

9th Bde (A?)
The Royal Scots

Place	Date	Hour	Summary of Events and Information	Remarks and references to Appendices
DOULLENS	7.3.16		The Battalion remained in Billets at DOULLENS	J.S.
IVERGNY	8.3.16		The Battalion paraded at 8.30 a.m. and marched with the Brigade to IVERGNY (via HAUTE VISÉE 13 of BREVILLIERS 4 of LE SOUICH - about 15 miles) where it billeted for the night	J.S.
MARŒUIL	9.3.16		The Battalion paraded at 8.45 a.m. and marched independently to MARŒUIL which it reached about 4.30 p.m. - a distance of 20 miles - and went into Billets - the route taken was via BEAUDRICOURT, road junction 'x roads just North of N in WARIN, AVESNES, HABARCQ, road junction just North of S in LA RESSET, ETRUN. The following Officers joined for duty :- MAJOR RATF MONCREIFF, CAPT. A. TAYLOR, CAPT. G.H.GREEN and CAPT. T.W. BENNETT CLARK - Carrying out fatigue Parties for the Brigade were provided.	D
ETRUN	10.3.16		The Battalion left MARŒUIL at 6.15 p.m. and marched to ETRUN (1 mile) where it went into Billets and who in respect to the 152nd th Infantry Brigade -
S. Howie Capt (Adj).
9th Royal Scots	J.S.

1875 Wt. W593/826 1,000,000 4/15 J.B.C. & A. A.D.S.S./Forms/C. 2118.

Army Form C. 2118

WAR DIARY
or
INTELLIGENCE SUMMARY

(Erase heading not required.)

9th Bn (Hhs)
The Royal Scots.

Instructions regarding War Diaries and Intelligence
Summaries are contained in F. S. Regs., Part II.
and the Staff Manual respectively. Title Pages
will be prepared in manuscript.

Reference Maps:
FRANCE SHEET 11 1/100,000
TRENCH MAP 1.S.1.3 N.W.1 1/10,000

Place	Date	Hour	Summary of Events and Information	Remarks and references to Appendices
ETRUN	11.3.16 to 15.3.16		The Battalion remained at ETRUN in reserve — and furnished working and carrying parties for the trenches, by day and night. On 12th his Observancho died from suffocation due to gas fumes from a coke brazier — On 14th 1 Otherrank was wounded by shrapnel bullet and admitted to hospital and 2 Other ranks were slightly wounded and transferred to duty — Chaplain the Revd. W.W. BEVER, DCS were transferred to 700th Infantry Brigade	12
TRENCHES	16.3.16 to 22.3.16		On the evening of 16th the Battalion relieved the 7th A.&S.Hhs in the trenches of the right sector (1) the Division being — 4 and B Companies being in the front line. C Coy in support and D Coy in reserve — HQ were at INODTON — The front trenches held were trenches taken over from the French by the Brigade they consisted mostly of advanced posts with supporting points behind. Relief complete from Square 22 B 60.15 & 6 22 B 1.7 (about 300 yards) we there join the right f and the 752 in.	J.Bruce Carter Lt.Col. 9th Royal Scots

WAR DIARY

or

INTELLIGENCE SUMMARY

(Erase heading not required.)

Instructions regarding War Diaries and Intelligence Summaries are contained in F.S. Regs., Part II and the Staff Manual respectively. Title Pages will be prepared in manuscript.

Army Form C. 2118

9th Bn (Glos)
The Royal Scots

IV

Place	Date	Hour	Summary of Events and Information	Remarks and references to Appendices
TRENCHES	16.3.16 to 22.3.16		Infantry Brigade. (51st Division) were on the left. The fire trenches and ammunition within trenches were left in very good repair by the French and an enormous amount of work was done in clearing them, making the parapet bullet proof, making firesteps and traverses and making the fire trenches and support line. Euro gun emplacements and support line. Euro gun emplacements and supply roads were also made. The enemy are comparatively quiet and here ... The front trenches we can't shell owing to their close proximity. The enemy were not shelled owing to their close proximity. but a good number of trench mortar bombs and rifle and hand grenades were fired by the enemy without doing much damage. Our trench mortar battery always silenced him. A reinforcement Draft (the 8th) ... the 9th Draft of 30 other ranks and a reinforcement Draft (the 8th) and 21 of September. Joined for duty on the 17th.	
			Casualties	
			17th. 1 O.R. killed by rifle fire	
			18th. 1 O.R. wounded (slightly) and returns to duty	
			19th. 2 O.R. killed by rifle fire	
			1 O.R. wounded by rifle fire	
			20th. 2 O.R. wounded by shell fire	

R. Bruce Capt (act)
9th Royal Scots

1875 Wt. W593/826 1,000,000 4/15 J.B.C. & A. A.D.S.S./Forms/C. 2118.

Army Form C. 2118

WAR DIARY

or

INTELLIGENCE SUMMARY

(*Erase heading not required.*)

Instructions regarding War Diaries and Intelligence
Summaries are contained in F. S. Regs., Part II.
and the Staff Manual respectively. Title Pages
will be prepared in manuscript.

9.A.13.(d) The Royal Scots

Place	Date	Hour	Summary of Events and Information	Remarks and references to Appendices
TRENCHES & ECURIE	22.3.16 to 28/3/16		On the night of 22/28th the Battalion was relieved by the 7th A.& H. Hrs and relieved the 4th SEAFORTH HRs and DIVISION'L CYCLISTS in Trenches ECURIE and ABRI CENTRALE (a large support about sq. 28.A.0.4.) A Coy was in the cellars at ECURIE and B Coy were in dugouts in Summerfield in sq. 27.A. and C and D Coys were at ABRI CENTRALE - these were the reserve line and was strongly fortified - occupying a command within over the surrounding country - and garrisoned by A.B. and C Coys and D Coy was in reserve. the right subsectn (L I) of the Brigade line held by the 4th SEAFORTH HRs and DIVISION'L CYCLISTS. During the six days at ECURIE the Batt'n was busily engaged putting the defences & the communication trenches in order, making dug-outs etc. the front at ECURIE was shelled daily, but no damage was done or any casualties sustained. On 21st inst the 5th reinforcing draft of 20 o.r. arrived at ETRUN & joined the Bn. at ECURIE on 23rd. Relieved by C.L. Brown from the Bn. on 24th inst.	ℛ.

ℛ. |
| TRENCHES | 28/3/16 to 31/3/16 | | On the night of 28/29th the Batt'n was relieved at ECURIE by the 7th A. & H. Highlrs from Lt. Scott. and occupied Lr sector in their stead. | OM. |

1875 Wt. W593/826 1,000,000 4/15 J.B.C. & A.   A.D.S.S./Forms/C. 2118.

A.S. Blair Lt. Col. Cmg 9th Bn. Scots

WAR DIARY

or

INTELLIGENCE SUMMARY

(Erase heading not required.)

9th Bn (Highland) Royal Scots

VI

Instructions regarding War Diaries and Intelligence Summaries are contained in F. S. Regs., Part II. and the Staff Manual respectively. Title Pages will be prepared in manuscript.

Ref maps France 1/40,000 Trenches 57 D NE 1/10,000

Place	Date	Hour	Summary of Events and Information	Remarks and references to Appendices
TRENCHES	28/3/16 to 31/3/16		The front line – C on right of Sector Y & D on left – A Coy in support line & B Coy in reserve at ABRI de MOUTON. – HQ at MOUTON. The dispositions were much the same as on our previous occupation –(see entries for 16/3/16 to 22/3/16: and a great deal of work was done in putting the fire trenches etc in proper order. The enemy were comparatively inactive in our Sector, tho' they threw in a good number of trench mortar bombs, rifle grenades and occasionally shelled the back trenches and communication trenches, doing no damage. On night of 30/31st at 3.40 a.m. the enemy sprang a mine some distance away in our right and activity compelled (relieved) for 3/4 hours during which [illegible] (Re 10th) of 29 men S.I. officer ( ) joined for duty on 31st inst. Casualties since 30th inst – 21st 4 O.R. slightly wounded by trench mortar 30 1 O.R. killed by T.M. (pte M. while unner C.G.) " 4 O.R. wounded by T/m (since returning to duty)	AM W.S. Playfair Lt Col

1875 Wt. W593/826 1,000,000 4/15 J.B.C. & A. A.D.S.S./Forms/C. 2118.

Army Form C. 2118

11/ 9ᵗʰ Bⁿ (Tᵀ.) The
Royal Scots

11/ Rfh Snob
Trench map 51.B NW1 1/10,000

WAR DIARY
or
INTELLIGENCE SUMMARY

(Erase heading not required.)

Instructions regarding War Diaries and Intelligence
Summaries are contained in F. S. Regs., Part II.
and the Staff Manual respectively. Title Pages
will be prepared in manuscript.

Place	Date	Hour	Summary of Events and Information	Remarks and references to Appendices
TRENCHES	1-4-16 to 2-4-16		The Battalion continued in Subsectⁿ L2, the dispositions being as on 31-3-16 -	J.S.
	3-4-16		On the evening of 3ʳᵈ the Battalion marched in by the 7ᵗʰ A.&S.Hᵈ⁸ and went back to billets in ETRUN, where it became Divisional Reserve. Casualty 1 O.R. wounded -	J.S.
ETRUN	4-4-16 to 9-4-16		The Battalion remained in billets at ETRUN. A working party of 50 men was furnished daily for work on communication trenches - the remainder of the Battalion were engaged in cleaning up and general routine. On 6-4-16, 2ⁿᵈ Lt W CAMPBELL joined for duty. On the night of 9/10ᵗʰ the Battalion relieved the 7ᵗʰ A.&S.Hᵈ⁸ in L2 Subsectⁿ. A Amᵈ B Coy being in the front line, D Coy in support and C Coy in reserve. The 4ᵗʰ GORDON Hᵈ⁸ were on the right and the 152ⁿᵈ Brigade on the left.	J.S.
TRENCHES	10-4-16 to 15-4-16		The dispositions of the Bⁿ remained as on night of 9/10ᵗʰ. The enemy were comparatively quiet and inactive. Now no rifle fire and machine gun fire were occasional, but their artillery showed certain J.Brice Ardragh Lt Col Royal Scots	

1875 Wt. W593/826 1,000,000 4/15 J.B.C. & A. A.D.S.S./Forms/C. 2118.

Army Form C. 2118

WAR DIARY

or

INTELLIGENCE SUMMARY

(*Erase heading not required.*)

Instructions regarding War Diaries and Intelligence
Summaries are contained in F. S. Regs., Part II.
and the Staff Manual respectively. Title Pages
will be prepared in manuscript.

Place	Date	Hour	Summary of Events and Information	Remarks and references to Appendices
TRENCHES	10-4-16 to 15.4.16		activity. During fortnight 15th/16th The Battn were relieved in Subsecln L₂ by the 7th A.S.Hrs and relieved the 7th SEAFORTHS Hrs at ECURIÉ. B Coy being in the dug-outs at the Railway Embankment in C Coy in the cellars and dug-outs in ECURIÉ, A Coy at ABRI CENTRALE and B Coy went to billets in ÉTRUN and dug-outs. A large amount of work was done in improving all trenches and making dug-outs. Casualties — on 11th. — 3 OR wounded (1 to duty) 12th. — 1 OR wounded accidentally 13th. — 1 OR wounded returned to duty	J.L.
ECURIÉ	16-4-16 to 21-4-16		The dispositions of the Battalion remained as on evening of 15th inst. and during this period the Battalion was engaged in work on the ECURIÉ defences under the R.E. On the evening of 21st the Battalion relieved the 7th A.S.Hrs in L₂ subsectn being in the front line. B Coy in support and A Coy in reserve.	J.L.
TRENCHES	22 April to 27-4-16		The Battalion continued to hold L₂ subsectn, the 4th Gordon Hrs being on the right, and the 153rd L.B. on the left. The dispositions remained the same except	

J. Smar Calder (?) Lt Col
9th Seaforth Hrs

1875   Wt. W593/826   1,000,000   4/15   J.B.C. & A.   A.D.S.S./Forms/C. 2118.

Army Form C. 2118

Ref: No?
France - Second Army 51.8. Nwi tioua (Naval Bn.)

9th Bn (Yr) The Loyal North Lancs

III

WAR DIARY
or
INTELLIGENCE SUMMARY
(Erase heading not required.)

Instructions regarding War Diaries and Intelligence Summaries are contained in F. S. Regs., Part II. and the Staff Manual respectively. Title Pages will be prepared in manuscript.

Place	Date	Hour	Summary of Events and Information	Remarks and references to Appendices
TRENCHES	22.4.16 to 27.4.16		For some shelling of the Front line & support line - On the 22nd Major W. GREEN D.S.O. 1st Bn The Black Watch joined the Battn for duty, and a draft of 26 O.R. also joined for duty. On 23rd Lt Col F. WESTMORLAND Cmr. G. D.S.O. Royal WARWICKSHIRE Regt (Res. of Officers) joined the Battalion. On 24th Lt Col A.S. BLAIR, C.M.G. relinquished command of the Battn on appointment as Commandant, ABANCOURT and Lt Col WESTMORLAND assumed the command. A draft of 48 O.R. joined for duty on 25th inst. On the evening of 2/3th inst the Battalion was relieved in "L2" subsector by the 7th A.S.Hrs. and marched to billets in ETRUN -	T.I.
			Casualties - on 24th - 3 O.R. wounded	
			- 26th - 2 O.R. wounded.	
ETRUN	29.4.16 to 30.4.16		The Battalion remained in billets as 154th I.B. and R.E. and 154th I.B. The weather during April was changeable; heavy rain about the middle of the month caused many cases of influenza. Mustard troubles - Otherwise the health of the Battalion was good. The ground was good.	

T.I. Westmorland Lt.Col
Commanding 9th Bn Royal Scots

1875 Wt. W593/826 1,000,000 4/15 J.B.C. & A. A.D.S.S./Forms/C. 2118.

WAR DIARY

or

INTELLIGENCE SUMMARY

(Erase heading not required.)

Instructions regarding War Diaries and Intelligence Summaries are contained in F.S. Regs., Part II. and the Staff Manual respectively. Title Pages will be prepared in manuscript.

FRANCE 1.41NS 1/100,000
TRENCH MAP. 51B N.W.1. 1/10,000

Vol 15 I

Place	Date	Hour	Summary of Events and Information	Remarks and references to Appendices
ETRUN	1.5.16 to 2.5.16		The Battalion remained in billets in ETRUN.	I.J.
TRENCHES	3.5.16 to 8.5.16		The Battalion relieved the 7th A.T. Ifs. in L2 Subsection on the Evening of 3rd inst. A and B Coys being in the front line and C in support and D in reserve. The 4th GORDONS were on our right and the 153rd Infantry Bde on our left. The period was comparatively quiet except on the afternoon of 5th inst when the front line was fairly heavily shelled with light shells and some H.E. The casualties for this period were:-	
			3rd Killed 1 O.R.	
			4th wounded at duty 2 O.R.	
			5th wounded accidentally 2nd Lt. J.R. BLACK	
			wounded 4 O.R.	
			wounded at duty 1 O.R.	
			6th wounded accidentally 1 O.R.	
			(accidentally)	
			8th wounded at duty 1 O.R.	
			On 7th inst, Lt. E.S. FIDDES joined for duty.	Lt Col (signature) L.S. Comdg 9th Royal Scots

1875   Wt. W593/826   1,000,000   4/15   J.B.C. & A.   A.D.S.S./Forms/C. 2118.

WAR DIARY
or
INTELLIGENCE SUMMARY
(Erase heading not required.)

Army Form C. 2118

9th B"C"(T/G) The
Payne Lords.

II

Instructions regarding War Diaries and Intelligence
Summaries are contained in F. S. Regs., Part II.
and the Staff Manual respectively. Title Pages
will be prepared in manuscript.

Place	Date	Hour	Summary of Events and Information	Remarks and references to Appendices
ECURIE	9.5.16 to		On the Evening of 9th the Battalion was relieved by the 7th K.A.& S.Hs in L 2 subsection and relieved the 4th SEAFORTH HRS at ECURIE - A Coy occupied the dugouts and B Coy the cellars. D Coy being at A1324 CENTRALE as C Coy in Brigade Reserve at ETRUN. A reinforcement of 49 O.R. joined for duty.	S.I.
- do -	10-5-16 to 14-5-16		The Battalion remained at ECURIE where it was engaged in work on the defences of this place.	S.I.
TRENCHES	15.5.16		On the afternoon of 15th the Battalion relieved the 7th K.A.& S.Hs in L2 subsector, who occupied ECURIE - C and D Coys were in the Front line. A Coy in Support and B Coy in Reserve - D. Col. P.T. WESTMORLAND on appointment to command 751st Infantry Brigade relinquished command of the Battalion and Major W. GREEN assumed command.	
	16.5.16	8.10 P.M.	At 8.10 P.M. the right battalion of the 152nd Infantry Bde on our left assisted by the Artillery made a raid on the enemy trenches opposite. Our Lewis Guns and snipers cooperated successfully and prevented the enemy from opening fire with his machine guns or rifles. Enemy artillery did very little firing on our trenches and were very quiet. Casualties - 2nd Lt. W. CAMPBELL wounded slightly at duty (self inflicted) wounded 1 O.R.	S.I.

Ref. Maps:
TRENCH MAP 51 B NW, 1/18000

Army Form C. 2118

9th (Scot.) The Royal Scots

WAR DIARY

or

INTELLIGENCE SUMMARY

(Erase heading not required.)

III

Instructions regarding War Diaries and Intelligence
Summaries are contained in F. S. Regs., Part II.
and the Staff Manual respectively. Title Pages
will be prepared in manuscript.

Place	Date	Hour	Summary of Events and Information	Remarks and references to Appendices
TRENCHES	17.5.16 to		The Battalion continued in its subsector. The enemy were fairly active and shelled the communication trenches freely, and on the 18th and 21st sent over a large number of trench mortars considerably damaging our trenches. We continually retaliated the enemy being in front up to	
	21.5.16		the enemy's lines. On 18th — 1 O.R. killed. On the afternoon of 21st. Coy was relieved by 4th Seaforth Hdrs. and "B" Coy By 4th Gordon Hdrs., the Divisional Front having been relieved to the North and the Brigade having to hold a large Front — these Coy proceeded to billets in ÉTRUN.	A.2.
			Casualties — 18th. Killed (Rec) 2 O.R.	
			Wounded (as) 4 O.R.	
			21st. do 4 O.R.	
			do (at duty) 2 O.R.	
			Wounded (as) 2 O.R.	
	22.5.16		The remaining Coys (A & D) were relieved during the day evening by 7th K.O.S.B. and on relief marched to ETRUN where the Battalion became Divisional Reserve	A.3.
ÉTRUN	23.5.16 to		The Battalion remained in Divisional Reserve and was employed in Brigade and R.E. fatigues. It also carried out training as far as possible, and	
	26.5.16		particularly the grenadiers, such as bombers, snipers and signallers —	A.3.

1875   Wt. W593/826 1,000,000 4/15 J.B.C. & A. A.D.S.S./Forms/C. 2118.

Comdg. 9 R.S.

WAR DIARY
or
INTELLIGENCE SUMMARY
(Erase heading not required.)

Army Form C. 2118

Instructions regarding War Diaries and Intelligence Summaries are contained in F. S. Regs., Part II. and the Staff Manual respectively. Title Pages will be prepared in manuscript.

Place	Date	Hour	Summary of Events and Information	Remarks and references to Appendices
	23.5.16 to 26.5.16		On 23rd inst. a draft of 58 O.R. of the 12th Royal Scots was attached to the Bn. for duty. On 25th inst. 1 O.R. was killed and 4 O.R. were wounded and returned to duty, through the accidental bursting of a rifle grenade at the Bde Grenade School. On 26th inst a draft of 4 O.R. of the 2nd The Royal Scots was attached for duty. On the afternoon the Battalion relieved the 7th A.I. Bn in the trenches. The method of working the Divisional front having been changed, the front of the 154th Inf. Bde was extended to the left to Sq A16 c. 32.62, joining with the 153rd Inf. Bde at that point. The front taken over by the Battalion extended from that front to French L 28 (Sq A226.2.2) where it joined the 4th Gordons on the right of the Brigade. A "B" and "C" Coys were in the front line with "C" Coy in support and "D" Coy of 4th Seaforth Hrs in Reserve. Bn. H.Q. was at POSTE L142 E (Sq A2.86.596)	
TRENCHES	29.5.16 to 31.5.16		The Battalion remained in the trenches and the general was comparatively quiet though the Enemy had periodic bursts of activity with French minnenwerfers and shells. A considerable amount of work was done in improving and strengthening the trenches. On the whole	

[signature]
Lt Colonel
Comdg 9th Batn R.S.

Army Form C. 2118

Ref. No. S.I.B.N.I. 1/10/10

9th (Service) Rifle Brigade

WAR DIARY
or
INTELLIGENCE SUMMARY
(Erase heading not required.)

Ⅴ

Instructions regarding War Diaries and Intelligence Summaries are contained in F. S. Regs., Part II. and the Staff Manual respectively. Title Pages will be prepared in manuscript.

Place	Date	Hour	Summary of Events and Information	Remarks and references to Appendices
TRENCHES	29-5-16 to 31-5-16		and the healthy the battalion are satisfactory — the morale are good. On 31st inst a strength of 17 O.R. prior for duty:- Casualties:- 29th Wounded ... 1 O.R. do. (at duty) 1 O.R. 30th do. do. 2nd A.E. Carison 6 1 O.R.	I.J. Lieut.Colonel Comdg 9th Rifle Brigade

1875 Wt. W593/826 1,000,000 4/15 J.B.C. & A. A.D.S.S./Forms/C. 2118.

JUNE 1916

WAR DIARY

or

INTELLIGENCE SUMMARY.

(Erase heading not required.)

Army Form C. 2118.

Instructions regarding War Diaries and Intelligence Summaries are contained in F. S. Regs., Part II. and the Staff Manual respectively. Title pages will be prepared in manuscript.

Ref. Map:
Trench Map 51B. N.W.1 1/10,000

Vol 16

Place	Date	Hour	Summary of Events and Information	Remarks and references to Appendices
TRENCHES	1-6-16 to 3-6-16		The Battalion continued in Subsectors No. 2 and on 3rd inst were relieved by the 7th A.S.H'rs in the Subsectors and relieved the 4th Suffolk H'rs in ECURIE. Two Coys the Battn were in reserve to No. 2 Subsector (Coy A Coy) and one Coy to No. 7 Subsector, the remaining Coy being part of the Permanent Garrison of ECURIE. On the 3rd inst A Coy 12th Royal Scots was attached for duty. Casualties: 1 OR 12th Royal Scots killed, 1 OR attached, wounded 1 OR, wounded of Duf, 2 OR 1 Capt 9th R.S Haddon R.A D.D wounded, 1 Capt DAR HADDON Princs Jack wounded at Duty. Capt DAR HADDON Princs Jack	
ECURIE	4-6-16 to 9-6-16		The Battalion remained as on 3rd inst and were employed in work on the defences of the line. The following seven officers joined for duty on 6 inst. Lieut N. D. WARDROP, 2nd Lt J. F. WILLIAMSON, A. M. A. MOIR, P. M. ROSS, R. GIBSON, and R. M. JAMIESON. On 9th inst between 3 and 5 from the Battalion relieved the 7 Royal Scots in No. 2. B. Greenfield Lt Col	

2353   Wt. W2544/1454   700,000   5/15   D. D. & L.   A.D.S.S./Forms/C. 2118.

WAR DIARY
or
~~INTELLIGENCE SUMMARY~~
(Erase heading not required.)

Army Form C. 2118.

Instructions regarding War Diaries and Intelligence
Summaries are contained in F. S. Regs., Part II.
and the Staff Manual respectively. Title pages
will be prepared in manuscript.

Place	Date	Hour	Summary of Events and Information	Remarks and references to Appendices
EcuRie	4-6-16 to 9-6-16		Anberton, A.B and C. Coys being in the Front line and D. Coy in support. Two Coys of 7th H.L.I. were in reserve. Casualties: 4th: Wounded — 1 O.R 7th: Killed — 1 O.R 12th R.I. ant? Killed — 1 O.R. Wounded — 1 O.R. Wounded at duty — 1 O.R.	A.9.
TRENONES	10-6-16 to 15-6-16		The Battalion remained in No 2 subsector. The Division was comparatively quiet though the enemy had been more active and between 3.30 and 4.30 pm on 15th shelled the Support line fairly heavily doing some damage to the trenches. On the afternoon of 15th the Battalion was relieved by the 7th Argyll and Sutherland Hdrs and proceeded to Etrun, as Divisional Reserve. On 12th not a draft of 3 O.R. joined. Casualties: 11th — wounded 2 O.R. wounded at duty 1 O.R. 12th — wounded dead 3 O.R. 15th — wounded 1 O.R. [2nd Lt C.L Brown and 1 O.R.]	A.9.

2353   Wt. W2544/1454   700,000   5/15   D. D. & L.   A.D.S.S./Forms/C. 2118.

Ref. Draft
Finished M of. S - B N W I I/100 vo.

WAR DIARY

or

INTELLIGENCE SUMMARY.

(Erase heading not required.)

Instructions regarding War Diaries and Intelligence
Summaries are contained in F. S. Regs., Part II.
and the Staff Manual respectively. Title pages
will be prepared in manuscript.

III

Place	Date	Hour	Summary of Events and Information	Remarks and references to Appendices
ETRUN	16-6-16 to 21-6-16		The Battalion remained in Divisional Reserve in ETRUN and was engaged during this period in fatigue work under R.E. and Brigade. Training was also carried out by Companies and by Lewis Gun teams Snipers and Bombers. A draft of 35 Other ranks joined for duty on 20th inst. Casualties - killed 1 OR. wounded 1 OR. On the afternoon of 21st the Battalion relieved the 7th R.S.W.Bs in Right Sub-Section. B Coy being on the right C Coy in the Centre and A Coy in support. The 11th Suffolks were on the right and 153rd Infy Bde on the left.	J.S.
TRENCHES	22-6-16 to 25-6-16		The disposition of the Battalion remained as on afternoon of 21st. During the 25th 26th 27th and 28th inst our Artillery and Trench Mortars Batteries carried out a systematic bombardment of the German front and support lines. Doing considerable damage. The enemy reply was confined mainly to Field Gun shells. with	J.S.

Lt Gen ..... Comd Bn

WAR DIARY

or

INTELLIGENCE SUMMARY.

(Erase heading not required.)

Instructions regarding War Diaries and Intelligence
Summaries are contained in F. S. Regs., Part II.
and the Staff Manual respectively. Title pages
will be prepared in manuscript.

Place	Date	Hour	Summary of Events and Information	Remarks and references to Appendices
TRENCHES				

[Handwritten summary of events — partially legible:]

Some 4.2 and 5.9 howitzer shells. Aeroplane was active mainly on our communication trenches between Support and firing lines. On snipers cooperated. Shots on Snap in Snap were very quiet. On night of 23/24 enemy were active on enemy Snap, succeeded in capturing one man. On evening of 28th the Battalion was relieved by 9th A.S.I. Hrs in Right Sub-sec. and placed at Wulverghem in EaRiE. A and B Coys being in Reserve & Night 2 subsecs. D Coy to Right One 2nd Cdy being part of garrison of EaRiE. On 27th inst Major A.G.N. de BERRY, 13th H.L.I. was attached for duty.

Casualties:

Date			Other Ranks	Unit
22	Wounded		3	O.R.
23	do (at duty)		1	O.R. 12th/R.S. attached
	do.		2	O.R.
24	Missing (?prisoner)		1	O.R.
25	Killed		2	O.R.
	Wounded		2	O.R. 12th R.S. attached
26	Killed		1	O.R.
27	do		–	O.R.
	Wounded		2	O.R.
	(at duty)		2	O.R.

[signature]

2353 Wt. W2544/1454 700,000 5/15 D. D. & L.   A.D.S.S./Forms/C. 2118.do

Army Form C. 2118.

WAR DIARY
or
INTELLIGENCE SUMMARY.
(Erase heading not required.)

Instructions regarding War Diaries and Intelligence
Summaries are contained in F. S. Regs., Part II.
and the Staff Manual respectively. Title pages
will be prepared in manuscript.

Ref: Map 51 B N.W.1 1/40,000
France 51.B 1/40,000

V

Place	Date	Hour	Summary of Events and Information	Remarks and references to Appendices
Ecurie	29 and 30.6.16		The Battalion remained as on August of 28th June and on afternoon of 30th was relieved by units of the 60th Division as follows :- B and D Coys by 2 Coys 2/21st LONDON REGIMENT and A and C Coys by 2 Coys 2/22nd LONDON REGIMENT. HQ remained by HQ 2/22nd LONDON REGIMENT. One officer and 4 N.C.O's per Coy remained behind for instructional purposes. On relief the Battalion proceeded by march route to MAROEUIL where it went into Reserve. The health of the Battalion and the remainder was good.	S.d.

for proper J. Lt Col
Comdg 9 Bn/148 The Royal Scots |

2353   Wt. W2514/1454   700,000   5/15   D. D. & L.   A.D.S.S./Forms/C. 2118.

154th Brigade.

51st Division.

1/9th BATTALION

THE ROYAL SCOTS.

JULY 1 9 1 6

Vol 17

1.7 R.S.

CONFIDENTIAL

WAR DIARY

OF

9TH BATTN (HRS) THE ROYAL SCOTS.

FROM _____ 1ST July _____ TO _____ 31ST July _____

Ref. hope.
[?] Inf.a 61 - NW 1 1/10000
France : 51.B and C.

9th Batt. The Royal Scots.
Army Form C. 2118.

I

WAR DIARY

or

INTELLIGENCE SUMMARY.

(Erase heading not required.)

Instructions regarding War Diaries and Intelligence Summaries are contained in F. S. Regs., Part II and the Staff Manual respectively. Title pages will be prepared in manuscript.

Place	Date	Hour	Summary of Events and Information	Remarks and references to Appendices
MAROEUIL	1-7-16 to 4-7-16		The Battalion remains in Reserve and on afternoon of 4th relieved 7th A. & S. Hrs. in Right 2 Subsector: the distribution being C & D and A Coys in Right Centre and Left areas respectively and B Coy in support. The 4th Gordon Hrs. were on the right and 153rd Infantry Bde on the left. On 2nd a draft of 34 O.R. joined for duty.	S.D.
TRENCHES	5-7-16 to 10-7-16		The Battalion remains in Right 2 Subsector. From 4/5 to 6/7 July the Left half Battalion 2/22nd London Regiment was attached for instruction and the Right half Battalion 2/21st London Regt. from 7/8 to 9/10th July. On 5th Lieut. Hon. BALLINGALL, 6th Bn. the Royal Scots, joined for duty. On 10th the Battalion was relieved by 7th A. & S. Hrs. and marched to billets in ÉTRUM. Casualties : 5th Wounded. 6th Wounded. 1 O.R. 2 O.R.	S.D.

B. Brown.
Lt. Col.
Comdg. 9th Royal Scots |

2353 Wt. W2544/1454 700,000 5/15 D.D.&L. A.D.S.S./Forms/C. 2118.

Ref: Inst:
Ref: Sheet 11

WAR DIARY
or
INTELLIGENCE SUMMARY.

(Erase heading not required.)

Instructions regarding War Diaries and Intelligence Summaries are combined in F. S. Regs., Part II. and the Staff Manual respectively. Title pages will be prepared in manuscript.

Place	Date	Hour	Summary of Events and Information	Remarks and references to Appendices
ETRUN	11-7-16 to 12-7-16		The Battalion remained in Divisional Reserve and carried out training. Beside doing fatigues for R.E. and Brigade.	L.9
CHELERS	13-7-16 to 14-7-16		On the morning of 13th the Battalion marched to billets in CHELERS, a distance of about 12 miles, where it arrived about 1.40 p.m. On 13th 2nd Lt J.D.COWAN and this reinforcement draft of 50 and 76 joined for duty. The latter was composed of 6th 8th and 70th Royal Scots and 8th Highland Light Infantry. The Battalion remained in CHELERS on 14th.	L.9
LE SOUICH	15-7-16	At 2.30pm.	on 15th the Battalion marched from CHELERS to road junction 200x S. of first E in TINQUETTE then E from where it was carried by motor lorries to LE SOUICH where it billeted for the night.	L.9
BEAUMETZ	16-7-16	At 7.5 am	the Battalion left LE SOUICH and marched to LE MEILLARD where the Battalion proceeded by NEUVILLETTE, BARLY, MEZEROLLES to BEAUMETZ (a distance of about 15 miles) where it arrived about 1.35 pm and went into billets.	L.9
	17-7-16 to 19-7-16		The Battalion remained in billets and carried out training. B.Green Lt. Col. Comdg. 9th Royal Scots	L.9

2353   Wt. W2544/1454 700,000 5/15 D.D.&L.   A.D.S.S./Forms/C. 2118.

WAR DIARY
or
INTELLIGENCE SUMMARY.
(Erase heading not required.)

Army Form C. 2118.

III

Instructions regarding War Diaries and Intelligence
Summaries are contained in F. S. Regs., Part II.
and the Staff Manual respectively. Title pages
will be prepared in manuscript.

Ref Map
62 D N.E, & 57c. S.W.

Place	Date	Hour	Summary of Events and Information	Remarks and references to Appendices
MÉAULTE	20·7/16		The Battalion left BEAUMETZ abt 1·30 am and marched to CANDAS (about 6 miles) where it detrained for MÉRICOURT. After detraining at MÉRICOURT the Battalion marched via BRAY to MÉAULTE (about 5 miles) where it arrived about 2·30pm and went into Billets — The Battalion moved to IV Corps South Army — The Transport proceeded by road from BEAUMETZ from 19·7·16 about 7·45 pm and rejoined the Battalion about 8 pm on 20·7·16	
Trenches BAZENTIN LE GRAND WOOD.	21/7/16		The Battn. paraded at 6·15pm. and moved off at 6·15pm via FRICOURT and MAMETZ to trenches in the vicinity of BAZENTIN LE GRAND WOOD. The Coys. were disposed as follows :— D Coy & A in front line — WINDMILL S 9 c S·8 to S 9 c O·8.; Half A Coy in strong point at S9c 11·3 B & C Coys in reserve at S.W. edge of BAZENTIN LE GRAND WOOD. Twenty officers only were taken into action with the Battn. The others remained at Transport Lines.	P.J.G.S.
	22/7/16		The Battn. held trenches as above. Transport moved to vicinity of BÉCORDEL. xxxxxxxxxxxxxxxxxxxxxxxxxxxxxxxxxx	Lt Col Comdg 9th R.S.

Instructions regarding War Diaries and Intelligence
Summaries are contained in F. S. Regs. Part II
and the Staff Manual respectively. Title pages
will be prepared in manuscript.

WAR DIARY

or

INTELLIGENCE SUMMARY.

(Erase heading not required.)

9ᵗʰ Battn. (Hrs) The Royal Scots

Army Form C. 2118.

Ref Map 57c S.W.

IV

Place	Date	Hour	Summary of Events and Information	Remarks and references to Appendices
Trenches	Night 22/23 7/16		The XIII, XV, & III Corps continued this attack. The objective of the 51ˢᵗ Div. was N.E. & N.W. Edges of HIGH WOOD, also Switch Trench from N.E. Edge of HIGH WOOD westward to M 33 d 4.0. Front allotted to 9ᵗʰ Royal Scots was S4 a. 1.8 — M 33 d. 4.0. 4 Gordon Hrs were on right.	
"	23/7/16		Inf. Assault began at 1.30 a.m. B.Y.C. Coys. carried out the attack. Front allotted as follows — B Coy S4 a 1.8. — S 3 b 7.8. Coy. S3 b 7.8.– M 33 d 4.0. The other officers in B Coy were Lt. WARDROP. H.M. Maj. F.B. MONCREIFF commanded B Coy. 2/Lt. F.B. MONCREIFF , 2/Lt R. GIBSON. Maj. R.H.F. MONCREIFF commanded C Coy. The other officers in C Coy. were Lt. A.N. BALLINGALL , 2/Lt. W.B. BENTLEY, 2/Lt. A.E.D. LYALL. The assaulting coys. were subjected to heavy shell fire while crossing open ground also to machine gun fire on reaching S 3 d. The two coys. lost touch with each other and also with the Battns. on right and left. Maj. MONCREIFF, Lt. BALLINGALL, Lt. WARDROP, 2/Lt. MONCRIEFF, 2/Lt. BENTLEY, & 2/Lt LYALL were wounded and brought back. Maj. FERGUSON and 2/Lt. GIBSON were also hit. Many of the N.C.Os and men became casualties, and the remainder	R.J.B.

P.J.B.

[signature]

Lt-Col.
Comdg. 9ᵗʰ R.S.

2353 Wt. W2544/1454 700,000 5/15 D. D. & L. A.D.S.S./Forms/C. 2118.

WAR DIARY

or

INTELLIGENCE SUMMARY.

(Erase heading not required.)

Instructions regarding War Diaries and Intelligence
Summaries are contained in F.S. Regs., Part II.
and the Staff Manual respectively. Title pages
will be prepared in manuscript.

Ref Map 57c S.N.

Place	Date	Hour	Summary of Events and Information	Remarks and references to Appendices
Trenches.	23/7/16		of the two coys, having become split up, returned to the trench from which they had stalled. Maj. FERGUSON and 2/Lt. GIBSON were found to be missing. The Battn. remained in original position. Capt. & Adjt. S. FRASER, Lt. MORRIS W.M. and 2/Lt. GELLATLY J.S. were wounded by shell fire. Casualty Return, in addition to officers noted above, now 22nd & noon. 28th killed 7 O.R.; wounded 89 O.R.; missing 66 O.R. In the evening the Battn. was relieved by 7th Argyll & Sutherland Hrs. and moved to Dugouts at MAMETZ WOOD. S 20 a 2.8.	P.9/08.
MAMETZ WOOD	24/7/16		This Battn. remained in Brig. Reserve in these dugouts. Carrying Parties were provided to take supplies and stores to Battn. in HIGH WOOD. Casualty Return Wounded 6 O.R., including one accidentally, one accidentally Missing one.	P.9/08.
"	25/7/16		2/Lt. F.T. DANIELS joined for duty — He remained at transport lines. Battn. situated as on 24th C Coy. was heavily shelled. 2/Lt. N. WARDROP received shell shock. Lt. W.T.P. SPENS was wounded slightly & returned to duty. Casualty Return wounded 3 o.R. slight.	P.9/08.

WAR DIARY
or
INTELLIGENCE SUMMARY.
(Erase heading not required.)

Instructions regarding War Diaries and Intelligence Summaries are contained in F.S. Regs. Part II. and the Staff Manual respectively. Title pages will be prepared in manuscript.

Ref Map 57c S.W. 62 d N.E.

Place	Date	Hour	Summary of Events and Information	Remarks and references to Amendices
MAMETZ WOOD.	26/7/16		Battn. was relieved at 4pm. by 7th Gordon Hrs. and marched to Bivouacs near BECORDEL. The Brig. was now in Divl Reserve. Casualty Return — (noon 25th - noon 26th) killed 7 OR. Wounded 24 OR.	p.98.
BECORDEL. (Bivouacs)	27/7/16		Battn. in Divl Reserve as above. Casualty Return — Wounded 1 OR.	p.98.
"	28/7/16		" " " " Draft of 105 O.R. arrived composed of 5th 6th R.S. 2nd 9th R.S. H.4 2/5 R.S. 13th 15th R.S. 1st R.S.F. 23rd HLI S.R. 1st, 2nd, 3rd, 4th, 12th, 15th, 16th, 17th, 19th H.L.I. Total Estimated casualty Return 21st to 9am 26th July :— Majors 2 Captains 1 Subalterns 9 O.R. 212 (Killed 26 Wounded 147 Missing 39)	p.98.
"	29/7/16		Battn. in Divl Reserve as above.	p.98.
"	30/7/16		Same as 29/7/16.	p.98.

(signature) Lt. Col.
Comdg. 9th Royal Scots.

Army Form C. 2118.

WAR DIARY

or

INTELLIGENCE SUMMARY.

(Erase heading not required.)

Ref. Map 57c S.W. 62.d. N.E.

VII

Place	Date	Hour	Summary of Events and Information	Remarks and references to Appendices
BIVOUACS BECORDEL	31/7/16		Brig. in Div. Reserve. Capt. J. ROWBOTHAM, 8th H.L.I. attached 8th R.S., joined & act temporarily as Senior Major with authority to wear badges of Major.	P.gb.
			Potherington. Lt Col Comdg. 9th Royal Scots.	

2353   Wt. W2511/1451 700,000 5/15   D.D.&L.   A.D.S.S./Forms/C. 2118.

154th Brigade.

51st Division.

1/9th BATTALION

THE ROYAL SCOTS

(Highlanders)

AUGUST 1 9 1 6

Army Form C. 2118.

CONFIDENTIAL

No 71(A)

9th Bn. (Hrs.) The Royal Scots

HIGHLAND DIVISION.

WAR DIARY

or

~~INTELLIGENCE SUMMARY.~~

(Erase heading not required.)

Instructions regarding War Diaries and Intelligence Summaries are contained in F. S. Regs. Part II. and the Staff Manual respectively. Title pages will be prepared in manuscript.

6887

Place	Date	Hour	Summary of Events and Information	Remarks and references to Appendices
Bivouacs MEAULTE	1/8/16		The Battn. was in Divisional Reserve until the 154th Inf. Bde. moved into support, relieving the 152nd Inf. Bde. at 4 p.m. The Battn. marched off and relieved the 6th Seaforth Hrs. in MAMETZ WOOD – in trenches and dugouts. The relief was complete by 6.45 p.m. The position of the Battn. was about S, 19, 8, 7, 6. Transport and Details moved to F.6.a.	P.gas.
MAMETZ WOOD	2/8/16.		While in this position the Battn. provided carrying parties for supplies for the 152nd Bde. which was now in the front line. It also supplied working parties for the R.E. 1 Coy. was employed daily for carrying – the other time for working. The strength state on reaching MAMETZ WOOD was officers 21, other ranks 645. Casualty Return Noon 1st to Noon 2nd O.R. wounded 12 (including one at duty).	P.gas.
"	3/8/16		As on 2/8/16. Casualty Return Noon 2nd to Noon 3rd O.R. wounded 5. Position was shelled by 4.2" & 5.9" Hows. from 3 p.m. To 4.30 p.m. Capt. G.D. COWAN was wounded	P.gas.
"	4/8/16		As on 3/8/16. Casualty Return Noon 3rd to Noon 4th killed O.R. 5, wounded O.R. 18.	P.gas.
"	5/8/16		" " 4/8/16 " " 4th " 5th " 4	P.gas.
"	6/8/16		" " 6/8/16 " " 5th " 6th wounded Lt. W.P.T. SPENS (6th) & O.R. 5. Missing O.R. 1. The position was shelled from 12.30 am from 7.4 am. In the afternoon the Battn. was relieved by the 4th in King's: The Division.	P.gas.

[signature] Lt. Colonel
Comdg 9th Royal Scots

2353   Wt. W25H/1454   700,000   5/15   D.D.&L.   A.D.S.S./Forms/C. 2118.

Army Form C. 2118.

Instructions regarding War Diaries and Intelligence Summaries are contained in F. S. Regs., Part II. and the Staff Manual respectively. Title pages will be prepared in manuscript.

WAR DIARY

or

INTELLIGENCE SUMMARY.

(Erase heading not required.)

Ref. Maps etc S.W. 8 62d N.E.

Place	Date	Hour	Summary of Events and Information	Remarks and references to Appendices
MAMETZ WOOD.	6/8/16		Being relieved by the 33rd Div. and the Bttn. by the 98th Inf. Bde. The Battns. relief was complete by 6.20 p.m. Bttns. moved independently to X Roads F.1.d.9.0 where the Battn. was formed up. The Battn. then marched to Bivouacs in D.1.18.F. The Transport and details had reached two days before in the morning; the march was via VIVIER MILL & DERNANCOURT. The Battn. arrived at 9.50 km. The Trench strength on leaving MAMETZ WOOD was — Officers 19, other ranks — 586. The number of men sent "dropped sick" while the Battn. was in MAMETZ WOOD was eleven. The Total number of casualties for period 21st July to 6th Aug. inclusive was:— Officers wounded 12, missing 2, other ranks:- Killed 32, wounded 210 (including 12 "slightly at duty") missing 44.	O.P.O.S. O.P.O.S.
Bivouacs near DERNANCOURT				
"	7/8/16		Battn. in Bivouacs at 3 hours notice for moving. The following draft of officers joined for duty:—	O.P.O.S.

6897

over

WAR DIARY

or

INTELLIGENCE SUMMARY.

(Erase heading not required.)

Ref. Map AMIENS. ABBEVILLE.

Instructions regarding War Diaries and Intelligence
Summaries are contained in F. S. Regs., Part II.
and the Staff Manual respectively. Title pages
will be prepared in manuscript.

Place	Date	Hour	Summary of Events and Information	Remarks and references to Appendices
Bivouacs near DERNANCOURT.	7/8/16		Lieut's. J.L.GUNN 5th R.S.; R.M. IRELAND 5th R.S., F.M. SCOTT 5th R.S., 2/Lieut's. M. PEACOCK 6th R.S.; W.B.R. MORREN 6th R.S.; W.P. NEILL 6th R.S.; A.S. MUIR 8th R.S., J.R.M. MACDONALD 9th R.S., J.R.TAIT 6th R.S.; A.R.P. McMILLAN 9th R.S.; J.R FALCONER 4th R.S.; J.E. HEWISON 4th R.S.;	P.gs.
	8/8/16		D.C. McEWAN 9th R.S.; H. SHIRLAW 9th R.S., J.M. SUTHERLAND 9th R.S. The Transport moved in Bde. to TOULAINVILLE, starting at 2.15 p.m. and arriving about 11 p.m. The Battn. remained in Bivouacs. 94 O.R. drafted from Royal Scots, R.S. Fusiliers and Sco. Rifles were returned to Base Depôt.	P.gs.
	9/8/16		The Transport entrained its march starting about 8 a.m. The Battn. paraded at 5.45 a.m. and marched to MERICOURT, where it entrained. It detrained at LONGPRÉ about 12.30 p.m. and marched to ERONDELLE (about 8 Kilometres) where it arrived about 3 p.m. The Battn. Bivouaced - with the exception of the Officers and a few details who were billeted. The Transport arrived about 9 p.m.	P.gs.
ERONDELLE	10/8/16		The Battn. remained at ERONDELLE. The rest of the Bde. were billeted at neighbouring villages. DIV. H.Q. was at PONT REMY.	690+
"				

W.D. Greig.
Lieut-Col.
Comdg. 9th Royal Scots.

2353   Wt. W2544/1454 700,000 5/15   D. D. & L.   A.D.S.S./Forms/C. 2118.

Army Form C. 2118.

WAR DIARY
or
INTELLIGENCE SUMMARY.
(*Erase heading not required.*)

IV

Instructions regarding War Diaries and Intelligence Summaries are contained in F. S. Regs., Part II. and the Staff Manual respectively. Title pages will be prepared in manuscript.

Ref. Map ABBEVILLE & HAZEBROUCK 5a.

Place	Date	Hour	Summary of Events and Information	Remarks and references to Appendices
ERONDELLE	11/8/16		The Division moved into IInd Army Area. The Battn. paraded at 3.30 a.m. and marched to PONT REMY Station; it had been preceded by its Transport. From here, starting about 5 a.m., the Battn. and Transport were conveyed by Train to STEENBECQUE where it arrived about 2.30 pm. The Battn. marched to EBBLINGHEM (about 12 kilometres) and billeted there.	P.90S.
EBBLINGHEM	12/8/16		The Battn. carried out training.	
"	13/8/16		The Battn. remained billeted at EBBLINGHEM.	P.90S.
"	14/8/16		Transport started at 3.30 a.m. and marched in Bde. to ARMENTIERES. The Battn. entrained at EBBLINGHEM about 10 a.m., and detrained in ARMENTIERES.	P.90S.
ARMENTIERES			at STEENWERCK. Thence the Battn. marched to billets in ARMENTIERES arriving about 2.15 pm. The Transport arrived about 7.30pm. The Bde. relieved the 3rd New Zealand Bde. in Divisional Reserve beginning its relief of the 1st New Zealand Division by the 51st Division.	694

[signature], Lieut. Colonel commdg. 9th Royal Scots.

2353 Wt. W2544/1454 700,000 5/15 D.D.&L. A.D.S.S/Forms/C. 2118.

692x

Instructions regarding War Diaries and Intelligence Summaries are contained in F. S. Regs., Part II. and the Staff Manual respectively. Title pages will be prepared in manuscript.

WAR DIARY
or
~~INTELLIGENCE SUMMARY.~~

(Erase heading not required.)

Map Ref. HAZEBROUCK 5a/100,000. 36 N.W.1/40,000.

Place	Date	Hour	Summary of Events and Information	Remarks and references to Appendices
ARMENTIERES	15/8/16		The 152nd Inf. Bde. relieved the 1st New Zealand Bde. in the Right Sector of the 1st Division's line on night 15th/16th. About 6.30 p.m. ARMENTIERES was shelled for half an hour. Four other ranks were wounded in billets. The Batn. relieved the AUCKLAND Battn. 1st NEW ZEALAND Bde in left subsector of the Right Sector. The Right Sector extended from I 5, a, 4, 7; to I 5, a, 4, 7. The left subsector extended from I 5, c, 2, 2, to I 5, a, 4, 7. The 1/4th Sea. Hrs. relieved the Batn. in reserve in the Subsidiary line; and the 1/7th A. & S. Hrs. relieved the Right subsector; the 1/4th Gor. Hrs. relieved the Batn. in Bde. Reserve in ARMENTIERES. The front line by platoon comprised (1) front line Breastworks, organized in "localities." (2) Support line. (3) S.S. line. (A) Strong points in rear. Right front with 2 platoons in support :- "D" Coy. "B" Coy. S.S. line and 2 Strong points (X & Y). "C" Coy. in reserve (1 Platoon in BUTTERNE FARM and 3 in Dugouts). Relief was complete at 12.15 a.m. The night was very quiet. On the 16th 2/Lt. H.F. SLAUGHTER joined for duty.	P.G.S.
TRENCHES.	16/8/16		Coys. were disposed as follows :- "A" Coy. left front with 2 platoons in support. There were no casualties - the day was very quiet. On night 16th/17th dispositions were altered as follows :-	P.G.S.

[signature] Lieut. Col.
Comdg. 9th Royal Scots.

2353   Wt. W2544/1454   700,000   5/15   D. D. & L.   A.D.S.S./Forms/C. 2118.

Army Form C. 2118.

WAR DIARY
or
INTELLIGENCE SUMMARY.

(Erase heading not required.)

9th Bn (H.S) The Royal Scots.

VI

Instructions regarding War Diaries and Intelligence Summaries are contained in F. S. Regs., Part II. and the Staff Manual respectively. Title pages will be prepared in manuscript.

Ref Maps Hazebrouck 5a. 1/40,000 & 36 N.W. 1/20,000.

Place	Date	Hour	Summary of Events and Information	Remarks and references to Appendices
ARMENTIERES TRENCHES	17/8/16		"D" "B" & "A" Coys now held the Front line in depth, each finding its own supports. "C" Coy was in Strong Points in rear. (1 Coy of the 1st Bn Gordon Hrs. ("in Subsidiary line") was available as Battn Reserve. There were no casualties 16 th /17 th ?	P/9 s.
"	18/8/16		Patrols were sent out on night 16 th /17 th to find suitable ground for sapping from in front and to reconnoitre the ground generally, and to find whether enemy was patrolling. Reports were made on ground and wire and no sign of enemy patrols were found. Work was carried out improving dugouts, fire steps, wire etc. Enemy machine guns were active by night, otherwise everything was very quiet. The trenches were held as above.	P/9 s.
"			Patrols were again out on night 17 th /18 th to examine ground. The day was quiet, at night the German machine guns were active as usual. There were no casualties.	P/9 s.
"	19/8/16		The situation remained unchanged. Patrolling and work were carried out. A few small shells fell in the Batln. area during the day. Lewis guns were active at night, as were the German machine guns. There were no casualties.	693 x P/9 s.

J Burnett Lieut Colonel Comdg 9th Bn Royal Scots.

2353 Wt. W2344/7454 700,000 5/15 D. D. & L. A.D.S.S./Forms/C. 2118.

WAR DIARY

or

INTELLIGENCE SUMMARY.

Instructions regarding War Diaries and Intelligence
Summaries are contained in F. S. Regs., Part II
and the Staff Manual respectively. Title pages
will be prepared in manuscript.

(Erase heading not required.)

Ref. Map HAZEBROUCK 5G. /20,000 & 36 N.W. 1/40,000.

Place	Date	Hour	Summary of Events and Information	Remarks and references to Appendices
ARMENTIERES Trenches.	20/8/16		The situation and work in the trenches continued as on previous day.	
"	21/8/16		2/Lt. J.F. WILLIAMSON rejoined for duty. There was no casualties. The day was quiet except for a few field gun shells fired by germans at Trench 76 without damage. The Battn. was relieved by the 9th Battn. A.&S. Hrs and went in to Bde. Reserve in Billets in ARMENTIERES. no casualties occurred during two tour in the Trenches.	P.yas.
ARMENTIERES Billets.	22/8/16.		The Battn. supplied working and carrying parties daily, while in Bde. Reserve. Training was carried out	P.yas.
"	23/8/16		As above. Four N.C.O.s joined for duty from Reserve Battn. to relieve similar number & to returned from france to the Home Establishment.	P.yas.
"	24/8/16		Working parties and Training as above	P.yas.
"	25/8/16		As on 24/8/16.	P.yas.

6944

W. Green
Lieut Colonel
Comdg 9th Royal Scots.

2353 Wt. W2544/1454 700,000 5/15 D. D. & L. A.D.S.S./Forms/C. 2118.

WAR DIARY

or

INTELLIGENCE SUMMARY.

(Erase heading not required.)

Instructions regarding War Diaries and Intelligence
Summaries are contained in F. S. Regs., Part II.
and the Staff Manual respectively. Title pages
will be prepared in manuscript.

Ref. Map HAZEBROUCK 5a.

Place	Date	Hour	Summary of Events and Information	Remarks and references to Appendices
Camp near BAILLEUL	26/8/16		The 152ⁿᵈ Inf. Bde. relieved the 154ᵗʰ in the Right Sector of the line. The 15ᵗʰ Seaforth Hˢ relieved the Battn. The 154ᵗʰ Bde. moved into Corps Reserve. On relief the Battn. started at 9 a.m., marched to a Training Camp 1 mile S.E. of BAILLEUL.	Appx.
"	27/8/16		There was a Church Parade together with the 4 Gordon Hrs.	Appx.
"	28/8/16		Training was carried out	Appx.
"	29/8/16		The G.O.C. the IIⁿᵈ Army presented Decoration Ribbons to members of the Division and afterwards inspected the 154ᵗʰ Bde., which then marched past. In the afternoon training was continued. The following was published in Bde. Routine Orders:— "The Brigadier General Commanding is directed to convey to all ranks of the 154ᵗʰ Inf. Bde. the satisfaction of Lᵗ Genᵉʳᵃˡ Sᵉʳ Herbert Plumer, Commanding Second Army, and Lieutenant General Sir Arthur Godley, Commanding IIⁿᵈ A.N.Z. Army Corps, at the good appearance, steadiness, and smartness on parade of the Bde. this morning. The Brigadier General is fully aware that the Brigade	Appx.

69 x

(Sgd)

Lieut Colonel
Comdg 9ᵗʰ Royal Seats.

2353 Wt. W²⁵⁴⁴/1454 700,000 5/15 D.D.&L.   A.D.S.S./Forms/C. 2118.

Army Form C. 2118.

WAR DIARY
or
INTELLIGENCE SUMMARY.
(Erase heading not required.)

Instructions regarding War Diaries and Intelligence
Summaries are contained in F. S. Regs., Part II.
and the Staff Manual respectively. Title pages
will be prepared in manuscript.

9ᵗʰ Bn (Hᵗˢ) The Royal Scots.

WW1 IX

Ref. Map HAZEBROUCK 5a 1/100,000.

Place	Date	Hour	Summary of Events and Information	Remarks and references to Appendices
Camp near BAILLEUL.	29/8/16.		will justify the on all occasions the task entrusted to him, by the Army Commander that "They are as good as any task".	PROS.
"	30/8/16		Training was carried out. A draft of 30 other ranks joined for duty.	PROS.
"	31/8/16		" " " "	PROS.

(Sgd)/. Lieut. Colonel
Comdg 9ᵗʰ Royal Scots.

696 +
58

2353   Wt. W2544/1454   700,000   5/15   D. D. & L.   A.D.S.S./Forms/C. 2118.

CONFIDENTIAL

WAR DIARY

9TH BATTALION (HIGHLANDERS) THE ROYAL SCOTS

FROM 1ST SEPT. 1916

TO 30TH SEPT. 1916

Army Form C. 2118.

WAR DIARY
or
INTELLIGENCE SUMMARY.

(Erase heading not required.)

9th Bn. (Hy.) The Royal Scots

I

Ref Map "HAZEBROUCK 5a" 1/100,000 or Sheet 36 N.W. 1/20,000

Part II 9 "HOUPLINES" Trench Map 1/10,000

Instructions regarding War Diaries and Intelligence Summaries are contained in F. S. Regs., Part II, and the Staff Manual respectively. Title pages will be prepared in manuscript.

Place	Date	Hour	Summary of Events and Information	Remarks and references to Appendices
Training Camp 1 mile S.E. of BAILLEUL.	1/9/16		Training was continued as on previous days.	P.Gs.
	2/9/16		In the morning training was carried out. At 1 pm, the Battn. marched to NIEPPE and PONT DE NIEPPE and billeted in these villages. The Battn. relieved the 70th Inf. Bde. in Divisional Reserve for the 23rd Division, coming under the orders of the 9th Corps.	P.Gs.
NIEPPE	3/9/16		In the afternoon the Battn. relieved the 12th D.L.I. in the Right subsector of the front line of the 23rd Division — the Bde. relieving the 68th Inf. Bde. in the line. The Battn's front extended from C. 16, d, 7, 4 to C.4, a, 6, 0. "A", "B" & "C" Coys. held the front line from right to left "D" Coy. was in support line. Relief was reported complete at 5.30 pm. The right was quiet.	P.Gs.
Trenches North of River Lys,	4/9/16		About 2.45 pm. a considerable number of Trench Mortar bombs were fired by Enemy in D Battn Area. Some damage was done, but there were no casualties. Our Trench Mortars fired later, and were replied to by the Enemy. Casualty Return - Nil. 30 other Ranks joined for duty from Base Depot.	P.Gs.

W. Wem
Lieut Col.
Commdg. 9th The Royal Scots.

2353   Wt. W2544/1454 700,000 5/15   D. D. & L.   A.D.S.S./Forms/C. 2118.

Instructions regarding War Diaries and Intelligence
Summaries are contained in F. S. Regs. Part II.
and the Staff Manual respectively. Title pages
will be prepared in manuscript.

WAR DIARY
or
INTELLIGENCE SUMMARY.
(Erase heading not required.)

Ref Map 36 N.W. 1/20,000
and Intelligence "HOWLINE" Trench Map 1/10,000

Place	Date	Hour	Summary of Events and Information	Remarks and references to Appendices
TRENCHES NORTH OF RIVER LYS.	5/9/16		Day quiet, except that about 4.30 p.m. three large Trench mortar Bombs were fired into "A" Coy area - two men were killed. At night a patrol was out to reconnoitre ground in front between "CARTER'S FARM" and the LYS.	1/9th.
"	6/9/16		Day quiet, in the evening our artillery was active. Captain W.E.S. LINDSAY and two other ranks ("slightly at duty") were wounded. The ground in front of "CARTER'S FARM" was again patrolled at night.	1/ Gas.
"	7/9/16		from 4.30 p.m. to 6.30 p.m. our artillery was active; about 5 p.m. enemy retaliated with numerous Mortar Bombs on "C" & "D" Coy areas, 2 other ranks wounded "D" Coy relieved "A" Coy in Right Front Patrolling was carried out at night in front of the Right Coy	1/ gas.
"	8/9/16		The Bde. was relieved by the 58th Inf. Bde. The Battn. was relieved by 9th Welch Regt. Relief was completed by 1.30 p.m. The Battn. marched to billets in ARMENTIERES. The Bde. rejoined the 51st (High.) Division.	1/ gas.

64 x

B. Green
Lieut Colonel
Comdg. 9th Royal Scots

2353 Wt. W.2541/1454 700,000 5/15 D. D. & L.   A.D.S.S./Forms/C. 2118.

Army Form C. 2118.

WAR DIARY
or
INTELLIGENCE SUMMARY.

(Erase heading not required.)

Ref. Map 36 N.W. 1/20,000 HOUPLINES 1/10,000.
Trench Map

Instructions regarding War Diaries and Intelligence
Summaries are contained in F. S. Regs., Part II.
and the Staff Manual respectively. Title pages
will be prepared in manuscript.

9th Bn (H.S.) The Royal Scots

III

Place	Date	Hour	Summary of Events and Information	Remarks and references to Appendices
ARMENTIERES TRENCHES (HOUPLINES)	9/9/16		The Bde. relieved the 153rd Inf. Bde. in Left Sector of 57th Div. Front. The Battn. relieved the 5th GORDON H'rs. as "C" Battn. in the Subsidiary line. Relief was complete at 11.15 a.m. Coys were from right to left :- "C" "D" "B".	PJS.
"	10/9/16 to 14/9/16		Carrying and working parties were furnished for the R.E. about 200 men. Being supplied daily. On 13th Casualty Return 1 O.R. wounded "slightly at duty".	PJS
	15/9/16		The Battn. relieved the 9th A.& S. H'rs. in the Right Subsector of the front line. Relief was completed before midday. Coys were disposed in the front line from right to left "B" "C" "D" with "A" Coy in support. On the night 15th/16th/16 there were two raids on the German Trenches opposite the Left Sector organised by the 153rd Inf. Bde. that from the right of the Battn. by the 9th Gordon H'rs. the other from its left of/the of the Battn. by the 7th Black Watch, the other from its left/ of the Battn. by the 9th Gordon H'rs. Zero time for these raids was 8.55p.m. The former was successful. The latter unsuccessful owing to a failure to cut its wire. During the day previously arranged schemes of artillery and	PJS.

700x

(signature) Lieut. Colonel
Comdg. 9th Royal Scots

WAR DIARY

or

INTELLIGENCE SUMMARY.

(Erase heading not required.)

Instructions regarding War Diaries and Intelligence
Summaries are contained in F. S. Regs., Part II.,
and the Staff Manual respectively. Title pages
will be prepared in manuscript.

Ref Map 36 N.W. 1/20,000

9th Bn. (Hrs) The Royal Scots

IV

HOUPLINES 1/10,000

Trench Map 2/3

Place	Date	Hour	Summary of Events and Information	Remarks and references to Appendices
HOUPLINES (trenches)	16/9/16		Trench Mortar fire were carried out against the Enemy's wire and trenches with good effect. During the night 15th/16th two other ranks were	P/Gs.
			killed and two wounded (one slightly at duty) by German retaliation. a draft of nine other ranks joined from Base Depot.	
			During the day Artillery and T.M. Bombardment scheme was continued	
			at night a Raid was carried out by the Battn. from the Left subsector	
			of the Right sector. The Raiding Party was composed of 9 — Lieut.	
			A.H. Douglas — in command — 2/Lt F.M. Ross , six N.C.Os and 27 men. The	
			party left Trenches at I, 5, c, 35, 26, at 8·10 pm. The German wire and	
			Trenches were bombarded by Artillery and Trench Mortars starting at 8·39pm.	P/Gs
			The party meanwhile halted into position and advanced at 8·45pm. Lieut.	
			A.H. Douglas was killed on enemy parapet, and 2/Lt Ross was wounded.	
			He however assumed command and reorganised the party which had	
			become confused. The party entered Enemy Trench — the Germans	
			vacating it on arrival of the party, after bombing the party as it advanced	
			through the wire. A machine gun emplacement was bombed — various	
			articles of clothing and equipment were removed from shelters. Three	
				787

10th June Lieut.Colonel
Comdg 9th Royal Scots

WAR DIARY
or
~~INTELLIGENCE SUMMARY.~~
(Erase heading not required.)

Instructions regarding War Diaries and Intelligence
Summaries are contained in F. S. Regs., Part II.
and the Staff Manual respectively. Title pages
will be prepared in manuscript.

Ref Map 36 N.W. 1/20,000

HOUPLINES

Trench Map

10,000

9th Bn. (Hrs.) The Royal Scots.

V

702 ×

Place	Date	Hour	Summary of Events and Information	Remarks and references to Appendices
HOUPLINES Trenches.	16/9/16		Germans were killed for certain and more casualties were reported. The casualties of the party in addition to the officers mentioned were 16 other ranks wounded. The wire party returned to the British trenches bringing the body of Lt. Douglas with it. One other rank was wounded in the trenches on this date.	ggs.
"	17/9/16		The situation continued as before – no activity except for trench mortar firing by both sides – no casualties.	ggs.
"	18/9/16		As on 17th. The task of German artillery fire was almost entirely confined to trench mortars on our side. The enemy's aggression stokes guns, rifle grenades and trench guns were used to harass suspected enemy working parties.	ggs.
"	19/9/16		Situation and conditions unchanged – patrolling carried out at night to reconnoitre "Nomans land" and german line. – one other rank wounded.	ggs.
"	20/9/16		The day was quiet as before – one other rank wounded. Patrolling carried out as above.	ggs.
"	21/9/16		No event of importance occurred, the Trenches were held as above.	ggs.

[signature] Paul Glass

Adjg. 9 R. Scots

2353 Wt. W2544/1454 700,000 5/15 D. D. & L. A.D.S.S./Forms/C. 2118.

Army Form C. 2118.

WAR DIARY

or

INTELLIGENCE SUMMARY.

(Erase heading not required.)

Instructions regarding War Diaries and Intelligence
Summaries are contained in F.S. Regs. Part II.
and the Staff Manual respectively. Title pages
will be prepared in manuscript.

Ref Map 36 N.W. 1/20,000
Hooplines Trench map
1/10,000.
HAZEBROUCK 5a. and LENS 11.

9th Bn. (H.S.) The Royal Scots
VI

Place	Date	Hour	Summary of Events and Information	Remarks and references to Appendices
Hooplines Trenches	22/9/16		The 154th Lt. Fds. was relieved by the 8th Argyll Suff. Bn. The Battn. was relieved by "A" Battn. Gordon Regt. Relief was completed at 11 a.m. The Battn. marched to Erquinghem. A draft of five stars ranks joined for duty from its Base.	?yos.
Erquinghem Billets	23/9/16		The Battn. was billeted in Erquinghem	?yos.
	24/9/16		as above. Joint Church Parade with 9th Argyll Suff. H.Pds.	?yos.
Estaires Billets	25/9/16		The Bole marched to killed in Estaires in the morning.	?yos.
"	26/9/16		The Army Commander (1st Army) saw the Bole on the march & a route march by the whole Bole through Neuf Berquin was arranged for this purpose.	?yos.
	27/9/16		Training was carried out = Battn. remained billeted at Estaires	?yos.
	28/9/16		As on 27th inst.	?yos.
	29/9/16		as on 27th inst. A draft of eleven other ranks joined for duty.	?yos.
	30/9/16		The Battn. and Transport marched to Merville station and entrained at 10 a.m. The detraining station was Candas when the Battn. arrived about 5.30 p.m. from Merville. The Battn. and Transport marched to Candas village and billeted there.	?yos.

2353 Wt. W2511/1454 700,000 5/15 D. D. & L. A.D.S.S./Forms/C. 2118.

J Rowbotham Major
for Lieut Colonel
Comdg 9th Royal Scots

Vol 20

20 R.S.

CONFIDENTIAL

WAR DIARY

9TH BATT. (HIGHRS) THE ROYAL SCOTS

FROM 1ST OCT.

TO. 31ST OCT.

WAR DIARY
or
INTELLIGENCE SUMMARY.

Instructions regarding War Diaries and Intelligence Summaries are contained in F. S. Regs. Part II. and the Staff Manual respectively. Title pages will be prepared in manuscript.

Place	Date	Hour	Summary of Events and Information	Remarks and references to Appendices
CANDAS Billets.	1/10/16		The Battn. was billeted in CANDAS. The Division was now in the Reserve Army.	P.98.
"	3/10/16		as on 1st inst. Training was carried out	P.98.
FAMECHON Billets.	7/10/16		The Battn. marched in B.Co. to FAMECHON, starting at 9.45 am. and arriving about 2.45 pm. Bn. H.Q. were at SARTON. The Division joined the XIIIth Corps.	P.98.
BUS-LES-ARTOIS Billets.	4/10/16		The Battn. marched in Bde. to BUS-LES-ARTOIS The Battn. was billeted in huts outside Bus. 2/Lt. A.F. CAMERON joined for duty.	P.98.
"	5/10/16		Training was carried out. 2/Lt. C.H. ROSSILLARD 5th R.S. joined for duty.	P.98.
"	6/10/16		Training continued.	P.98.
"	7/10/16		as on 6th	P.98.
COLINCAMPS Bivouacs.	8/10/16		The Bde. relieved the 152nd Inf Bde in the line. The Battn. relieved the 5th Seaforth Hrs. in Reserve in Bivouacs at COLINCAMPS, arriving about 2 p.m. The Transport remained at Bus. One Battn. of the Bde. (4th Gordon Hrs) was in Trenches (K. 23, a, 7, 4 & K, 23, d, 1, 2). Carrying parties were provided for Tunnelling Stores and Trench Mortar Amn	P.98.
"	9/10/16		In Bivouacs - Carrying parties provided	P.98.

(signed)
Lieut. Colonel
Comdg 9th Royal Scots

2353   Wt. W2544/1454   700,000   5/15   D.D.&L.   A.D.S.S./Forms/C. 2118.

Ref Map LENS II 57 D 1/40,000
57 D S.W. 1/20,000
HEBUTERNE Trench map. 1/10,000

WAR DIARY

or

INTELLIGENCE SUMMARY.

(Erase heading not required.)

1/9th Bn. (Hrs.) The Royal Scots.

II

Instructions regarding War Diaries and Intelligence Summaries are contained in F. S. Regs., Part II. and the Staff Manual respectively. Title pages will be prepared in manuscript.

Place	Date	Hour	Summary of Events and Information	Remarks and references to Appendices
COLINCAMPS Bivouacs.	10/10/16		Carrying parties provided as on previous days.	P.gos.
"	11/10/16		As above	P.gos.
"	12/10/16		The Bde was relieved by the 153rd Inf Bde. The Battn was relieved by the 9th Black Watch about 5pm and marched to Billets at LOUVENCOURT. Carrying parties were supplied as before, previous to the relief.	P.gos.
Billets LOUVENCOURT.	13/10/16		Training carried out	P.gos.
"	14/10/16		Training continued. Draft of 115 other ranks joined for duty.	P.gos.
"	15/10/16		Training continued	P.gos.
"	16/10/16		do a do	P.gos.
FORCEVILLE (Camp).	17/10/16		The Battn marched to Camp at FORCEVILLE — The Transport also moved to there from BUS. Draft of 48 other ranks joined for duty from Bus.	P.gos.
LEALVILLERS Bivds.	18/10/16		The Battn with Transport marched to LEALVILLERS, arriving about 12.20pm. The Bn was all billeted there. 70th Regt. was now there also.	P.gos.
"	19/10/16		Training was carried out.	P.gos.

W. Green.
Lieut Colonel
Cmdg 9th Royal Scots.

9th Battn. (Hrs.) The Royal Scots

Army Form C. 2118.

WAR DIARY

or

INTELLIGENCE SUMMARY.

(Erase heading not required.)

Instructions regarding War Diaries and Intelligence Summaries are contained in F. S. Regs., Part II. and the Staff Manual respectively. Title pages will be prepared in manuscript.

111

Place	Date	Hour	Summary of Events and Information	Remarks and references to Appendices
LEFALVILLERS B.Hutts	20/10/16 22/10/16		Training continued.	P.Y.S.
MAILLY-MAILLET Bivouacs	28/10/16		The 164th Inf. Bde. relieved the 152nd Inf. Bde. in the Line. The Battn. relieved the 8th A.Y.S. Hrs. in Bivouacs in Wood P.18.c.8, near MAILLY-MAILLET - Relief was completed by 1.157pm.	P.Y.S.
"	23/10/16		Working and camping parties were provided for R.E. and Trench Mortar Batteries.	P.Y.S.
"	24/09/16		2 an 23rd	
"	25/09/16		A working party of 2 officers and 120 other ranks was provided for the 152nd Tunnelling Coy - being attached to it later for three days.	P.Y.S.
Trenches in front of AUCHONVILLERS	26/10/16		The Battn. relieved the 7th A.Y.S. Hrs. in the Trenches - The Battn. front was from Q.4,t, Q.65,0. & Q.10, t, 15.05. Relief was completed by 1.30am. Casualty return other ranks wounded.	P.Y.S.
"			The 7th A.Y.S. Hrs. attempted a raid from the Battn. front on the German Trenches, for the purpose of obtaining an identification - This raid was unsuccessful. "No mans land" and the enemy wire was reconnoitred.	

W. Fraser
Lieut. Colonel
Comdg 9th Royal Scots.

WAR DIARY or INTELLIGENCE SUMMARY.

(Erase heading not required.)

Instructions regarding War Diaries and Intelligence Summaries are contained in F. S. Regs., Part II. and the Staff Manual respectively. Title pages will be prepared in manuscript.

Place	Date	Hour	Summary of Events and Information	Remarks and references to Appendices
Trenches East of AUCHONVILLERS	27/10/16		There was a considerable amount of artillery fire on both sides during the night. Casualty:- Reltn:- other ranks five killed, three wounded (including one attd/y) Our artillery heavily bombarded the wire of the Enemy's BEAUMONT-HAMEL Section in the morning. In the afternoon Enemy shelled our support line heavily without much damage being caused. Patrolling of "No man's land" at night.	pgs.
"	28/10/16		Intermittent artillery fire continued during night, accompanied by our machine guns. Casualty:- Reltn:- one other rank wounded. Heavy bombardment by our artillery as on previous morning for 3 seconds often dire beginning 5:30 am. Several British aeroplanes active but no German. Patrolling at night to enemy front line. After return of patrols our mortars bombarded enemy lines with gas shells - Enemy replied with rifle and machine gun fire - followed by artillery.	pgs.
"	29/10/16		a/c 12.5 am fire on both sides reduced to an intermittent slow fire until unusual morning bombardment by our artillery at 6 a.m. with little reply until noon when Enemy guns shelled our front line. Relin:-Nart artillery and mortar fire continued. Throughout the day. Casualty. Relin. fire after reach corroded. Enemy artillery more active at night patrol found German front line wire badly broken and the trench much damaged, and unsuccessful for obstrue of 100 yards - The Patrol proceeded to Second line, examined wire there and returned unobserved.	pgs.

15[...].
Lieut Colonel.
Comdg 9th Royal Scots.

2353   Wt W2344/1454   700,000   5/15   D.D.&L.   A.D.S.S./Forms/C. 2118.

Ref Map 57D 1/40,000, 57 D.S.E. 1/20,000,   Army Form C. 2118.

Trench Map "BEAUMONT" 1/10,000.   9ᵗʰ Battⁿ (Highᵈ) The Royal Scots

V

WAR DIARY

INTELLIGENCE SUMMARY.

Instructions regarding War Diaries and Intelligence
Summaries are contained in F. S. Regs. Part II.
and the Staff Manual respectively. Title pages
will be prepared in manuscript.

(Erase heading not required.)

Place	Date	Hour	Summary of Events and Information	Remarks and references to Appendices
Trenches East of Puisieux.	30/10/16.		Artillery Bombardment of Enemy Trenches in morning unusual slow fire continued throughout the day. The Battⁿ. was relieved by the 6ᵗʰ Gordon Hⁱˢ - relief completed by 4.15ᵃᵐ. - and marched to billets in LEALVILLERS - Relⁿ. Hqᵖᵒ and two Battalion of the Rⁱᵗⁿ also moved to RAINCHEVAL - The 4ᵗʰ Suffolk Aᵗᵗ. were also billeted in LEALVILLERS. Transport of Rⁱᵗⁿᵗⁿ. also moved to there.	P72.
LEALVILLERS Billets.	31/10/16.		Battⁿ. remained billeted at LEALVILLERS.	P72.
"				

O.J. Turner.
Lieut Colonel.
Comdg 9ᵗʰ Royal Scots.

~ CONFIDENTIAL ~

Vol 21

WAR DIARY

9TH BATTALION (HIGHLANDERS) THE ROYAL SCOTS

FROM 1st November 1916

TO 30th November 1916.

Ref Maps 57D 1/40,000, 57D.S.E. 1/20,000

WAR DIARY

TRENCH MAP
"BEAUMONT" 1/10,000

INTELLIGENCE SUMMARY.

(Erase heading not required.)

Instructions regarding War Diaries and Intelligence
Summaries are contained in F. S. Regs., Part II.
and the Staff Manual respectively. Title pages
will be prepared in manuscript.

Place	Date	Hour	Summary of Events and Information	Remarks and references to Appendices
LEALVILLERS Billets.	1/11/16		The Battn. remained billetted at LEALVILLERS – Training carried out, and working parties for Road Repair and R.E. fatigues provided.	9/05.
"	2/11/16		Working parties for Road repair and R.E. fatigues of 220 other ranks provided. Training continued.	9/05.
"	3/11/16		As on 2d	9/05.
"	4/11/16		In addition to above parties 3 Officers and 150 other ranks were sent for work in forward area east of AUCHONVILLERS, 1 man was killed and four wounded on this party. Training was carried out by men not employed in above.	9/05.
MAILLY WOOD Bivouacs	5/11/16		The Battalion moved to Bivouacs in MAILLY WOOD in relief of the 9th Black Watch. The Transport moved to camp P.17.2. Part of B Coy remained at LEALVILLERS to train for a Raid	9/05.
"	6/11/16		Working and Carrying parties provided for R.E. and T.M. Batteries	9/05.
"	7/11/16		As on 6th working and carrying parties provided. at night a party under Captain A. TAYLOR (with 2/Lt J. BLACK, 2/Lt A.H. MOIR and 2/Lt IMMACLENNAN) of 52 of	9/05.
"	8/11/16		B Coy attempted a raid on the German trenches about Q.H.d.Q.2. The party was unsuccessful, failing to pass through the German wire x	9/05.

x owing to the heavy wire and difficult condition of the ground near it.

A.B. [signature]
Lieut Col
Comdg 9th Royal Scots

Instructions regarding War Diaries and Intelligence Summaries are contained in F. S. Regs., Part II. and the Staff Manual respectively. Title pages will be prepared in manuscript.

Ref. Map 57D 1/40,000 57D 8E 1/20,000 Trench Map "Beaumont" 1/10,000

9th Batn. (H.S.) The Royal Scots /II

Place	Date	Hour	Summary of Events and Information	Remarks and references to Appendices
MAILLY WOOD BIVOUACS.	7/11/16		were wounded and two were reported missing.	
TRENCHES EAST OF AUCHONVILLERS	8/11/16		The Battalion relieved the 7th A.&.S. Hrs. in the left sector of the King's "C"&"D" Coys were in the front line "A"&"B" in support. Relief was completed by 3/a.m. There was intermittent artillery firing throughout the day by both sides. Patrolling of No Man's Land was carried out at night. &/Lt. A. S. MUIR and one other rank were wounded.	gps. gps.
"	9/11/16		Artillery activity on both sides throughout the day. No Man's Land patrolled at night.	gps.
"	10/11/16		Bombardment of BEAUMONT HAMEL feebly replied to by our heavy Artillery from 5.20 a.m and 6 a.m. Casualty Return other ranks killed out, wounded five (including one accidentally)	gps.
"	11/11/16		A & B coys relieved C & D coys in the front line. Artillery active as usual. patrols at night examining the state of the present between our trenches and the German. Lewis peace active to prevent closing of gaps in wire.	gps.
"	12/11/16		Continued artillery activity. In the afternoon Battalion ofter 152nd and 153rd Inf. Bde. moved into the front trenches of the divisional "reserve in garrison to attack section.— The 153rd Bde. moved back to MAILLY-MAILLET. The Battalion on relief moved to camp in MAILLY. WOOD, the 137th Bde. being in reserve.	gps.

W. Breun.
Lieut Colonel
Comdg. 9th Royal Scots.

Ref BEAUMONT TRENCH Maps 1/10,000

57 D S.E. 1/20,000.

WAR DIARY
~and~
INTELLIGENCE SUMMARY.

(Erase heading not required.)

III

Instructions regarding War Diaries and Intelligence Summaries are contained in F. S. Regs. Part II and the Staff Manual respectively. Title pages will be prepared in manuscript.

Place	Date	Hour	Summary of Events and Information	Remarks and references to Appendices
MAILLY WOOD Camp	13/11/16		The Vth Army attacked on the morning of the 13th - the IInd Corps Rt of the ANCRE, the IInd Corps attacking at the same time on the South. Zero time was 5.45 am. The Divisions of the Vth Corps from Right to left were 63rd; 51st; 2nd; 3rd; the 37th was in Reserve. The 51st Division was ordered to capture BEAUMONT-HAMEL and push forward between the converging flanks of the 2nd and 63rd Divisions to "FRANKFORT TRENCH" Q.6,c,8,4 & Q.6,central, the 153rd Inf Bde attacked on the Right, the 152nd Inf Bde on the left. The 156th Inf Bde was in Reserve. The first stages of the attack of the division were entirely successful. The 152nd and 153rd Brigades captured the first four German lines including the village of BEAUMONT-HAMEL, meeting with after resistance and taking a number of prisoners.	P.J.B.
Operations at BEAUMONT-HAMEL	"	12.15pm	At 12.15 pm when the Battalion was waiting in readiness in MAILLY WOOD it was ordered to move into a position of assembly along the Railway line south of AUCHONVILLERS. HQ. was established at Q.8,d, central at 1.45 pm.	
"	"	1.45pm		

[signature] ~Lieut Colonel~
Comdg 9th Royal Scots.

2353 Wt. W2544/1454 700,000 5/15 D. D. & L.   A.D.S.S./Forms/C. 2118.

WAR DIARY

or

INTELLIGENCE SUMMARY.

(Erase heading not required.)

Instructions regarding War Diaries and Intelligence Summaries are contained in F. S. Regs. Part II and the Staff Manual respectively. Title pages will be prepared in manuscript.

Ref Trench Map "BEAUMONT" 57 D S.E. 1/10000 1/20,000

Place	Date	Hour	Summary of Events and Information	Remarks and references to Appendices
Operations at BEAUMONT-HAMEL	13/11/16	4.35 p.m.	at 4.35 p.m. A and D Coys were sent to reinforce the 153? Inf Bde. They moved up to "ST. JOHN'S ROAD" Q.16, 4, 2, 5. & Q.10, c, 5, 0.	P.90S.
		6.35 p.m.	at 6.35 p.m. The remainder of the Battn. also moved to the same position. The whole coming under the orders of the 153rd Inf Bde. Battn. HQ. was established with the HQrs 7th BlackWatch in "UXBRIDGE ROAD" Q.16, 4, 36, 50.	
"	14/11/16	1.15 am & 6 am	both early morning D Coy was sent to assemble at Q.17, 9, 1, 9 at 6 a.m. and to follow line of attack of 7ᵗʰ A9 S. Hrs. who were to attack FRANKFORT TRENCH. This attack did not take place. Capt Cowan receiving orders not to move from 157 ?Bln.	
"		7.44 am	A Coy moved to join D Coy. Capt. PABLAIR reported to Capt. R.D. COWAN at 12.15 p.m. Capt Cowan was ordered to move up "LEAVE AVENUE" and to bomb along "MUNICH TRENCH" working south. D Coy was however shelled out of the Battle and with Coys of the 7ᵗʰ A9 Hrs. put LEAVE AVENUE in a State of defence. Sabo Capt.	P.90S.
"	"	4 p.m.	COWAN reconnoitred "MUNICH TRENCH" which was now unoccupied by the enemy. In cooperation with R.E. 8ᵗʰ Royal Scots and 7ᵗʰ A9 Hrs. he dug the "NEW MUNICH TRENCH" and remained then, occupying it with his coy. until the following morning. A Coy meanwhile remained in BEAUMONT-HAMEL.	

[signature] Lieut. Colonel
Comdg 9ᵗʰ R. Scots.

Army Form C. 2118.

Ref Trench map "BEAUMONT" 1/10,000

WAR DIARY
or
INTELLIGENCE SUMMARY.
(Erase heading not required.)

9th Battn. (Hrs) The Royal Scots

V

Instructions regarding War Diaries and Intelligence 57D. SE. 1/20,000
Summaries are contained in F. S. Regs., Part II.
and the Staff Manual respectively. Title pages
will be prepared in manuscript.

Place	Date	Hour	Summary of Events and Information	Remarks and references to Appendices
Operations BEAUMONT-HAMEL.	15/11/16	4.45 am	Bn. H.Q. B and C Coys had meanwhile remained at "ST. JOHN'S ROAD". A Coy had remained at BEAUMONT-HAMEL. D Coy was relieved in NEW MUNICH TRENCH at 4.45 am and went back to BEAUMONT-HAMEL. In the afternoon A & D Coys returned to dugouts in "FETHARD STREET"	P.9os.
"	8/un		Q, 16, t, Bn. H.Q. moved into trenches in "FETHARD STREET" now vacated by Hqrs 1532 Inf Bde. B and C Coys moved into dugouts in V Ravine. The 4th Gordon Hrs. now occupied the Original 4th German line Q.11,d,6,8 & Q.11,b,1,9. B & C Coys were in Support to them.	
"	16/11/16		B and C Coys relieved the 4th Gordon Hrs in line Q.11,d, 6,8 & Q.11, b, 1,9 ; A & D Coys moved to the dugouts in V Ravine vacated by B & C Coys. On the right of B Coy was a Battalion of the 111th Inf Bde ; on the left of C Coy the 4th Seaforth Hrs.	P.9os.
"	17/11/16		The Battalion remained situated as on 16th. Trench occupied by B & C Coys was improved. As regards the position of the Battalion the situation was quiet all day.	P.9os.
"	18/11/16		A & D Coys relieved B & C Coys in the trench Q.11,d, 6,8, & Q.11, b, 1,9. Situation in Battn. Sector quiet.	P.9os.

Army Form C. 2118.

WAR DIARY
or
INTELLIGENCE SUMMARY.

(Erase heading not required.)

Instructions regarding War Diaries and Intelligence Summaries are contained in F. S. Regs., Part II. and the Staff Manual respectively. Title pages will be prepared in manuscript.

9th (Bdrs) The Royal Scots
VI.

Ref map "BEAUMONT" 1/10,000
57D. S.E. 1/20,000

Place	Date	Hour	Summary of Events and Information	Remarks and references to Appendices
Authuille BEAUMONT HAMEL.	19/11/16		The Batt. was relieved by the 5th Seaforth Hrs. and moved to Camps in MAILLY WOOD. During the operations since 13th Nov Casualties were Lieut R.M. IRELAND wounded (18th) other ranks killed 6, wounded 36 (including 3 at duty), died of wounds 1, missing 11. At the conclusion of the operations the line from the ANCRE northwards now passed through R,8,a,1,0, R,7,d,0,6, along BEAUCOURT Road to Q,6,e,5,3, eastwards to Q,5,d, central, thence northwards to K,35,c,5,6. BEAUMONT-HAMEL and BEAUCOURT-SUR-ANCRE had thus both been captured and the line advanced about one mile on an average along a mile frontage on the II Corps front.	P.J.S.
Camp MAILLY WOOD	20/11/16		Battalion remained in Camp at MAILLY WOOD	P.J.S.
	21/11/16		As in 20th	P.J.S.

[signature]
Lieut Colonel
Comdg 9th Royal Scots

2353 Wt W2544/1454 700,000 5/15 D.D.&L. A.D.S.S./Forms/C. 2118.

WAR DIARY
or
~~INTELLIGENCE SUMMARY~~

(Erase heading not required.)

9th Battn. (Hrs.) The Royal Scots
VII

Instructions regarding War Diaries and Intelligence Summaries are contained in F.S. Regs., Part II. and the Staff Manual respectively. Title Pages will be prepared in manuscript.

Ref Map 57D 1/40,000.

Place	Date	Hour	Summary of Events and Information	Remarks and references to Appendices
Camp MAILLY WOOD	22/4/16		The Battn. remained in Camp in MAILLY WOOD. A party of 4 officers and 200 other ranks was supplied for collecting salvage in the vicinity of BEAUMONT – HAMEL.	O/S.
Camp HEDAUVILLE	23/4/16		The Battn. and Transport moved to Camp at HEDAUVILLE, arriving about 10.30 a.m. The 51st Division was transferred from the 5th Corps to the 2nd Army.	O/S. O/S
Rich EBURG Battns.	24/4/16		The Battn. and Transport marched to billets in ROMMERCES, arriving about 1 p.m.	O/S.
	25/4/16		The Battn. remained billeted in ROMMERCES	
AVELUY HUTS.	26/4/16		The Battn. and Transport marched to Huts at AVELUY arriving about 5 p.m.	O/S. O/S
"	27/4/16		The Battn. remained in huts at AVELUY. A party of 1 officer & 100 other ranks was supplied for covering fights near OVILLERS	HZ.
OVILLERS HUTS	28/4/16		The Battn. (less transport & M.G.Sn.) marched to huts at OVILLERS arriving about 2 p.m. A party of 2 officers & 100 other ranks was supplied for covering fights near OVILLERS. The 2 M.G.Sns. moved to AVELUY	HZ.
"	29/4/16		The whole Battn. was employed in forwarding working parties.	RSR
"	30/4/16		The Battn. was employed as on the previous day. 10.R. wounded.	RSR

1875 Wt. W593/826 1,000,000 4/15 J.B.C. & A. A.D.S.S./Forms/C. 2118.

J.G. Brown
Lieut Colonel
Comdg. 9th Bn Royal Scots

~ Vol 22

CONFIDENTIAL

WAR DIARY

9th BATT (HIGHRS) THE ROYAL SCOTS

FROM 1/12/16

TO 31/12/16.

WAR DIARY

or

INTELLIGENCE SUMMARY

(Erase heading not required.)

L

1/5th Bn (Hus) The Royal Scots

Instructions regarding War Diaries and Intelligence Summaries are contained in F. S. Regs., Part II. and the Staff Manual respectively. Title Pages will be prepared in manuscript.

Reb Mah.

LE SARS 10/1066

Place	Date	Hour	Summary of Events and Information	Remarks and references to Appendices
TRENCHES	Nov/16			
OVILLERS HUTS	1/12/16		The Bn was employed in furnishing working parties. Casualties 1 OR killed 1 OR wounded.	A2.
"	2/12/16		The Bn was employed as on the previous day.	A2.
DUGOUTS W of COURCELETTE	3/12/16		The 154 Bde took over the line from the 152nd Bde. The Bn relieved the 6th R.H. in Supporting Position. W. of Courcelette, and were in dug out in R.29.a. Relief was reported complete by 10.30 h.m. Day was spent on a carrying party along LINS. Owing to the wet weather and the bad condition of the trenches however were much out of little.	A2.
"	4/12/16		The whole Bn were out on working parties.	A2.
"	5/12/16		As on previous day. Casualty 1 O.R. wounded.	A2.
TRENCHES	6/12/16		The Bn furnished a carrying party for the R.E. at 6 in morning, and at night took over the line from the 7th A.S.H. The relief was completed by 1.15. The Bn's sector was from M.13.b.2.4. to R.17.b.2.4. The line was held by 3 coys (A B & C - A being on the right - on the left), while D Coy was in support. Two platoons were detached from the Bn and lay between the Gunning Station R.99. & 6. 2 and the Sugar Factory R.36. A47. Casualties 2 O.R. killed 2 O.R. wounded.	A2.

(Signed) [signature]
Lt. Col. Commanding
5th Royal Scots

WAR DIARY
or
INTELLIGENCE SUMMARY

(Erase heading not required.)

Instructions regarding War Diaries and Intelligence Summaries are contained in F.S. Regs., Part II. and the Staff Manual respectively. Title Pages will be prepared in manuscript.

9th Bn. (H.D.) The Royal Scots   II

Place	Date	Hour	Summary of Events and Information	Remarks and references to Appendices
TRENCHES	7/12/16		Work was done at night to improving the trench by laying floorboards and erecting shelters. New trench also had to be dug in support - R.12.6. G.O.C. work was carried out here. Casualties. 2 O.R. wounded	62.
	8/12/16		As on previous day. The situation throughout the town in the trenches was unexceptional. 3 O.R. wounded	62.
OFFICERS HUTS	9/12/16		The Batt. was relieved by the 8th A.S.H. and marched to OFFICERS HUTS arriving there about 11.30pm.	39/2.
BILLETS BOUZINCOURT	10/12/16		The Batt. was relieved by the 7th Black Watch and marched to billets at BOUZINCOURT arriving there about 3.30pm.	39/25
Billets BOUZINCOURT	11-12-16 to 16-12-16		The Battalion remained in billets and provided working parties for brigade.	39/2
BRUGE HUTS AVELUY	16-12-16		The 151st I.B. went into support and the Battalion formed at 11am and marched to BRUGE HUTS near AVELUY (W.16 d 2.2) where it billeted (distance about 2 miles) - the Battalion provided working parties of 100 O.R.	39/2.
BRUGE HUTS AVELUY	17-12-16 to 20-12-16		The Battalion provided working parties - the huts were shelled at 11am and 6pm on 19th by H.V. Gun without damage - Casualties - 17th 1 O.R. wounded at duty. 18th 3 O.R. wounded.	39/2

[signature] — Lt. Col.
Comdg 9th Royal Scots

WAR DIARY
or
INTELLIGENCE SUMMARY
(Erase heading not required.)

Instructions regarding War Diaries and Intelligence Summaries are contained in F. S. Regs, Part II. and the Staff Manual respectively. Title Pages will be prepared in manuscript.

Ref. map 57 D 1/40000

III

1/9th Bn the Royal Scots

Place	Date	Hour	Summary of Events and Information	Remarks and references to Appendices
WOLFE HUTS & OVILLERS	21.12.16		The Battalion paraded at 8.45 A.m. and marched to WOLFE HUTS & OVILLERS HUTS (Support area) Bn HQ and A & B Coys being at the former and C and D Coys at the latter (Reserve area). The 152nd I.B. relieved the 153rd I.B. in the line.	J.G.
— do —	22nd/16 to 23rd/16		The Battalion remained at WOLFE HUTS and OVILLERS HUTS and provided working and carrying parties. On the evening of 23rd, the Lewis Guns (10) of the Battalion relieved the Lewis Guns of the 7th K.O.S.B. in the line.	D.G.
TRENCHES	24/7/16		Bn HQ. and Camp'd Coys relieved HQ. and 2 Coys of 7th K.O.S.B. in the front line of the Division during the evening. A and B Coys remaining in reserve at WOLFE HUTS. D Coy were on the right and C Coy on the left with 5 Lewis Guns to each, the front line being the same as on last form. One Coy (C) at A.I.Hqts at Bde H.Q. (R 29 central) and one Coy at CHALK MOUND (R 29 a 2.4) were in support.	D.G.
— do —	25/7/16 to 26/7/16		On 26th inst. the Lewis Guns were relieved on night of 26th by Lewis Guns of 8th A.S.Hqts (152nd Inf. Bde).	B.G.

B Green
Lt Col
Comdg 9th Royal Scots

WAR DIARY
or
INTELLIGENCE SUMMARY

(Erase heading not required.)

Instructions regarding War Diaries and Intelligence Summaries are contained in F.S. Regs., Part II. and the Staff Manual respectively. Title Pages will be prepared in manuscript.

IV

Ref. Map
L.B. CARS 1/2000
5/2/40,000

Place	Date	Hour	Summary of Events and Information	Remarks and references to Appendices
OVILLERS HUTS	27/7/16		The 1st & 2nd Bdes relieved the 154th. HQ. and 2 Coys 8th A.I.Mg relieved HQ. and 2 Coys in the front line which marched to OVILLERS HUTS for the night. A and B Coys marched to BOUZINCOURT where they billeted. A draft of 57 O.R. joined for duty. The 3 coys in the line were fairly quiet	S.S.
BOUZINCOURT	28/7/16		HQ. and C and D Coys marched from OVILLERS HUTS at 11 a.m. to BOUZINCOURT arriving about 12.30 p.m. where they billeted.	S.S.
- do -	29/7/16		A Quiet previous day. A draft of 35 O.R. joined for duty.	S.S.
- do -	30/7/16 6		The Battn remained at BOUZINCOURT. The health of the Battn was fairly good. Marching a certain amount of sickness owing to the weather which except for a few days at the beginning of the month, was wet.	S.S.
	31/7/16			

Breen Lt Col
Comdg 9th Royal Irish

Vol 23

CONFIDENTIAL

WAR DIARY

9th Battalion (Highlanders) The Royal Scots

From 1st January 1917

To 31st January 1917.

Army Form C. 2118

WAR DIARY
or
INTELLIGENCE SUMMARY

(Erase heading not required.)

Instructions regarding War Diaries and Intelligence Summaries are contained in F. S. Regs., Part II. and the Staff Manual respectively. Title Pages will be prepared in manuscript.

1/9 #2 Bn (1/9), The Royal Scots

57.0 1/4/0000

578 Bn

Place	Date	Hour	Summary of Events and Information	Remarks and references to Appendices
BOUZINCOURT	1·1·17 16		The Battalion remained in Billets at BOUZINCOURT – A draft of 56 O.Rs joined for duty on 1st and one of 6 O.Rs on 2nd.	D.J.
	2·1·17			
OUVILLERS HUTS	3·1·17		The Battalion left BOUZINCOURT at 10Am and marched to OUVILLERS HUTS where it arrived at 11·45 Am and went into support with Northumberland Brigade –	D.J.
OUVILLERS HUTS	4·1·17 16		The Battalion remained at OUVILLERS HUTS and provided working parties – CAPT W.C.S.LINDSAY and LIEUT W.I.R.SPENS joined for duty.	D.J.
	7·1·17		122 O.Rs joined for duty.	
TRENCHES	8·1·17		H.Q. and A and B Coys marched from OUVILLERS HUTS at 3·40 pm and relieves 1/7 and 2 Coys 9th A & S Hrs (153rd Infy Bde) in front line of O.3 Right section Divisional front line (M.15 A 5.5 to P.4 R.9 R.0 inclusive) A Coy on the right and 15 Coy on the left. the 15th Division III Corps being on our right and 7th A & S Hrs (154 the Infy Bde) on our left. B Coy was at M.19 3.7 8. One Company 4th Gordon Hrs were in support at FRASER'S POST (M.2.5 d- Sugar Trench) – E Coys and C Coy marched at same time to COURCELETTE DUGOUTS and Brewery at R.29 central respectively when they went into support to 7 K.A. & S Hrs –	D.J.
			No Casualties.	
			Com 9g the 9th Royal Scots	

1875 Wt. W503/826 1,000,000 4/15 J.B.C. & A. A.D.S.S./Forms/C. 2118.

Army Form C. 2118

WAR DIARY
or
INTELLIGENCE SUMMARY
(Erase heading not required.)

Instructions regarding War Diaries and Intelligence Summaries are contained in F. S. Regs., Part II. and the Staff Manual respectively. Title Pages will be prepared in manuscript.

Place	Date	Hour	Summary of Events and Information	Remarks and references to Appendices
TRENCHES	9-1-17		The Battalion remained as ommy at G.S. The line consisted of a series of posts with supporting posts and was much scattered. Our artillery conducted a bombardment of Enemy lines which often however, the Enemy being comparatively slight.	J.J.
WOLFE HUTS	10-1-17		H.Q. and A and B Coys were relieved by H.Q. and 2 Coys at G. of L. in the evening and marched to WOLFE HUTS. The bombardment by our artillery were continued during the day; the retaliation by the Enemy was greater than on 9th and front line were subjected to a heavy bombardment between 10 am and 12 noon and 2 to 2.45 p.m. — Carried B Coys remains on 9th. Reinforcing Officer (Capt G.S.G. STRACHAN, 2nd Bn R.C. BROWN and 2nd Lt H. S. SMITH) on 9th. The position of the H.Q. Battalion remained as on 10th — A draft of 8 ORs joined for duty.	J.J.
WOLFE HUTS	11-1-17		Carried B Coys were relieved by 6th Light Bn (2 on drum) the Enemy line marched to WOLFE HUTS. Were they rejoined the Battalion on relief.	J.J.
WOLFE HUTS	12-1-17		The Battalion was relieved by 6 to 6 of Sucks by dusk light Infy (5th Res) and moved to VAL DE MAISON at 6.45 pm. Were it arrived about 1 am in	J.J.
VAL DE MAISON	13-1-17		the Division. improvement by madin tram into the Div. was relieved by 2nd Division is not on spot.	J.J.

B. [signature]
Comdg 9th [Regt] C.S.O.

1875 Wt. W593/826 1,000,000 4/15 J.B.C. & A. A.D.S.S./Forms/C. 2118.

WAR DIARY
or
INTELLIGENCE SUMMARY

(Erase heading not required.)

Army Form C. 2118

Instructions regarding War Diaries and Intelligence Summaries are contained in F. S. Regs., Part II. and the Staff Manual respectively. Title Pages will be prepared in manuscript.

9th Bn Royal Welsh Fusiliers

Place	Date	Hour	Summary of Events and Information	Remarks and references to Appendices
FIENVILLERS	14-1-17		The Battalion marched with 154th Inf Bde at 12 noon and marched via TALMAS – LA VICOGNE – VERT GALAND FME – CANDAS – FIENVILLERS (about 11 miles) where it arrived about 4.15 p.m went into billets – asst of 8 O.Rs joined for duty.	S.1.
ONIEUX	15-1-17		The Battalion left FIENVILLERS at 8.30 a.m and marched via BERNEVILLE – FRANQUEVILLE – FRANSU – DOMQUEUR – LE PLOUY – ONIEUX (about 15 miles) where it arrived about 3 p.m went into billets. A draft of 9 O.Rs joined for duty.	S.1.
MORLAY	16-1-17		The Battalion left ONIEUX at 8.45 a.m. and marched (with the Northumberland) via ST RIQUIER – C. of MILLENCOURT – NEUILLY L'HOPITAL – NOUVION – PONTHOILE to MORLAY, where it arrived about 3.20 p.m – H.Q. and B Company billeted (about 16 miles) while A Company billeted in PONTHOILE.	S.1.
MORLAY	17-1-17 to 31-1-17		The Battalion remained in billets at MORLAY and PONTHOILE and went into training – the following reinforcements joined for duty on the 10th	S.1.

Cornd 9th Royal W. Fus.

1875 Wt. W593/826 1,000,000 4/15 J.B.C. & A. A.D.S.S./Forms/C. 2118.

WAR DIARY

or

INTELLIGENCE SUMMARY

(Erase heading not required.)

9th B.(Sr.) The Royal Scots

IV

Regmouth

Abbeville 1/100-00

Place	Date	Hour	Summary of Events and Information	Remarks and references to Appendices
MUTILAY	17.18.19/16		anto stated -	
	31.117		17th 2nd G. HUTTON , 3rd Royal Scots	
			19th 42 O.R.	
			21st { 2000 Lt. C. J AMIESON and 2nd Lt. J.A.W. ADAMS and	S.S.
			{ 53 O.R.	
			22nd 558 O.R.	
			The health of the Battalion was fairly good -	

Opinion - Lt. Col.
Comdg 9th Bn Royal Scots

Secret

War Diary

February - 1917 -

1/9ᵗʰ Bn. The Royal Scots (Hrs)

Army Form C. 2118

Instructions regarding War Diaries and Intelligence Summaries are contained in F.S. Regs., Part II. and the Staff Manual respectively. Title Pages will be prepared in manuscript.

9th B. "(Ho.) Northumb. Fus. Sous"

WAR DIARY
or
INTELLIGENCE SUMMARY

(Erase heading not required.)

Ref head: Abbeville 14.1/140,000

I

Place	Date	Hour	Summary of Events and Information	Remarks and references to Appendices
MORLAY	1/2/17 to 4/2/17		The Battalion remained at MORLAY and continued training	S.I.
LAMOTTE-BULIEUX	5/2/17		The Batt. left MORLAY at 1 p.m. and marched to LAMOTTE-BULIEUX (a distance of 12 kilos) via NOUVION arriving about 4 p.m., where it went into billets	S.I.
MARCH E-VILLE	6/2/17		The Batt. marched to MARCHEVILLE (about 8 kilos) where it arrived about 11 A.M. then went into billets	S.I.
BUIRE-AUX-BOIS	7/2/17		The Batt. marched to BUIRE-AUX-BOIS (about 22 kilos) via FRONVILLES - X roads about S. of FRONVILLES - X roads 200 x N.E. of REMONT - of FONTAINE-SUR-MAYE - NEUILLY-LE-DIEN - ACQUET - AUXI-LE-CHATEAU - leaving MARCHEVILLE at 8 A.M. arriving about 1.45 p.m. The Batt. went into billets	S.I.
BLANGER-VAL	9/17		The Batt. left BUIRE-AUX-BOIS at 9.30 a.m. and marched to BLANGERVAL (about 9 kilos) via ROUGEFAY and CONCHY, arriving about 11.45 went into billets.	S.I.

B. Trevor.
Lt. Col.
Comdg 9th Northumb. Fus.

1875 Wt. W593/826 1,000,000 4/15 J.B.C. & A. A.D.S.S./Forms/C. 2118.

WAR DIARY

or

INTELLIGENCE SUMMARY

(Erase heading not required.)

Instructions regarding War Diaries and Intelligence Summaries are contained in F. S. Regs., Part II. and the Staff Manual respectively. Title Pages will be prepared in manuscript.

9th Bn (H.) 9th Royal Scots

Place	Date	Hour	Summary of Events and Information	Remarks and references to Appendices
BAILLEUL	9-2-17		The Battalion left BLANGERVAL at 9 A.M. and marched via CROISETTE - CONCHY - ST POL - ROELLECOURT to BAILLEUL-SUR-CORNAILLES (about 22 kilos) where W.P. and A & C Coy billetted, B Coy moving on to CHELERS and D Coy billeting in TINCQUETTE.	S.S.
BAILLEUL	10-2-17		The Battalion remained as on 9th	S.S.
ECOURIES HUTS	11-2-17		The Battalion marched from its billets at BAILLEUL area and marched via SAVY - HAUTE AVESNES - ACQ to Huts at ECOURIES where it arrived at 2.45 p.m. The Bde was in Support to 152 - Iny Bde which was Both ouse on night of 11th in front of 9th Division lying between the ROELINCOURT - MAISON de la COTE ROAD (Sydnownes) and the LILLE ROAD (inclusive) -	S.S.
- do -	12-2-17 to 26-2-17		The Battalion remained as on 11th and provided working parties - The following reinforcements arrived for Batty on 16th 34 O.Ro, on 21st 60 O.Ro on 21st - 25th 15 O.Ro - Lieut W.T.P. SPENS died on 18-2-17 and 1 O.R. on 21st -	S.S.

Lt Col
Comdg 9th Royal Scots

WAR DIARY
or
INTELLIGENCE SUMMARY

(Erase heading not required.)

Instructions regarding War Diaries and Intelligence Summaries are contained in F. S. Regs., Part II. and the Staff Manual respectively. Title Pages will be prepared in manuscript.

Ref maps.
Kems II. 1/100,000
Part II. Rocurcourt.
51 : N.W1 1/19,000
iii

9th B (98th) The Royal Scots.

Place	Date	Hour	Summary of Events and Information	Remarks and references to Appendices
TRENCHES	27·2·16		The Brigade relieved the 152nd Inf Bde in the line, taking over the divisional front. The Battalion (less Lt. T. A. H. Lawson and 2 Lt. H. St. R. Law) proceeded to HERMIN for training) relieved the 4th Seaforths Hrs in the left subsector of the divisional front, the 6th Seaforth Hrs (152nd I. B.) being in right subsector, having been relieved by 154th I. B. The 28th Canadian Batt. was on the left. The right (inner) of the Battn. was on the right (BONNAL TRENCH) with 3 platoons, A Coy in the right front with 3 platoons. A Coy the left with 2 platoons (CORRECTEUR TRENCH). A Coy was on the left - Battn at LA SABLIERE. D being in the support line and B Coy in the support trench.	J.2.
- do -	26-2916		The Battn. remained as in 27/2 - wounded 1 OR. For the first half of the month the weather was very trying and for the latter half the front became very quiet. The health of the Battn. was fairly good. The morale good.	J.3.

(signature)
Lt. Col.
Comdg 9th R Highland Scots.

1875 Wt. W593/826 1,000,000 4/15 J.B.C. & A. A.D.S.S./Forms/C. 2118.

WAR DIARY
or
INTELLIGENCE SUMMARY
(Erase heading not required.)

Instructions regarding War Diaries and Intelligence Summaries are contained in F.S. Regs., Part II. and the Staff Manual respectively. Title Pages will be prepared in manuscript.

Ref map ROCLINCOURT 9B NW 1 1/10,000

Place	Date	Hour	Summary of Events and Information	Remarks and references to Appendices
TRENCHES	1-3-17		The Battalion Remained as on 28th Febry. Wounded 1 OR.	S.9
-do-	2-3-17		A and B Coys Relieved Canal D Coys respectively in the front line, the Battn occupying the positions in support vacated by A and B Coys. Wounded 1 OR.	S.9
-do-	3-3-17		The Battn remained as on 2nd inst. A draft of 12 ORs joins for duty. Killed on 3rd 2nd Lt J. R. M. MACDONALD.	S.9
-do-	4-3-17			
MAROEIL	5-3-17		The Battalion was relieved during the early evening by 4th Gordon Hrs and on relief marched to MAROEIL where it went into billets as Brigade Reserve. Killed 1 OR	S.9
-do-	6-3-17 to 10-3-17		The Battalion remained at MAROEIL and provided working parties under the R.E.s. Wounded on 6th 1 OR.	S.9
BOIS DE MAROEIL	11-3-17		The Battalion moved to Bois DE MAROEIL (2 kil.) and occupied huts vacated by 4th SEAFORTH HRS. Wounded 1 OR.	S.9
-do-	12-3-17 to 15-3-17		The Batt. remained at Bois DE MAROEIL under the R.E.s. A draft of 20 ORs joined for duty on 13th inst.	S.9

S. Routhorphson Major
Comdg 9th S. Seaforth

1875 Wt. W593/826 1,000,000 4/15 J.B.C. & A. A.D.S.S./Forms/C. 2118.

Army Form C. 2118

9th (S) (R) The Royal Scots

WAR DIARY
or
INTELLIGENCE SUMMARY

(Erase heading not required.)

Instructions regarding War Diaries and Intelligence
Summaries are contained in F. S. Regs., Part II.
and the Staff Manual respectively. Title Pages
will be prepared in manuscript.

Ref maps.
LENS 11 1/100,000
ROGLINCOURT FRENCH MAP 57B N.W.I 1/10,000

II

Place	Date	Hour	Summary of Events and Information	Remarks and references to Appendices
FREVILLERS	16-3-17		The Battn was relieved by 7th BLACK WATCH and marched to FREVILLERS (about 16 kils) leaving at 12.40 pm and arriving at 5 pm. Route:- ECOIVRES - ACQ - CAPELLE FERMONT - AGNIERES - MINGOVAL - BETHONSART.	S.J.
- do -	17.3.17 to 21-3-17		The Battalion remained at FREVILLERS and conducted attack practice. A draft of 20 joined for duty on 18th and a draft of 40 ORs joined for duty on 19th inst	S.J.
MAROEUIL HUTS	22-3-17		The Battalion left FREVILLERS at 10.30 am and marched to HUTS near MAROEUIL arriving about 2.30 pm (a distance of about 17 kils). Route:- BETHONSART - MINGOVAL - AGNIERES - CAPELLE FERMONT - ACQ - ECOIVRES - BRAY.	S.J.
ECURIE	23-3-17		The Battalion relieved 4th SEAFORTH HRS at ECURIE DEFENCES and came under orders of 153rd Infantry Bde - (in support) Dispositions; the A and D Coys and 3 platoons B Coy in ECURIE VILLAGE and Supports in sunken roads at A27 a - C Coy and 1 platoon B Coy in MN21N.	S.J.
- do -	24-3-17 to 31-3-17		The Battalion remained at ECURIE and worked on assembly trenches on left of Divisional Sector and practised carrying parties. The following casualties	

J. Rankastruing Major
for Lt Col Comdg 9th Royal Scots

Army Form C. 2118.

WAR DIARY
or
INTELLIGENCE SUMMARY.

(Erase heading not required.)

Instructions regarding War Diaries and Intelligence
Summaries are contained in F. S. Regs., Part II.
and the Staff Manual respectively. Title pages
will be prepared in manuscript.

Ref map. ROLINCOURT TRENCH MAP
51 B. N W 1 1/20,000

9th (S.S.) The Royal Scots

III

Place	Date	Hour	Summary of Events and Information	Remarks and references to Appendices
ECURIE	24·3·17 to 31·3·17		occurred during the period — 26th wounded ORs 2 wounded at duty OR1. 28th missing OR1 30th wounded at duty OR1. the following re-infor-cements joined for duty :- 26th, ORs 30, 27th, 2Lt A.C. SYKES 7th Royal Scots 2nd Lts D.R. FORSTER, H. COOK and A.F. WATSON, all 4th Royal Scots and 31st ORs 18. The health of the Battalion was on the whole good and was undermined only occasionally with occasional sickness of a minor nature. The morale good. The weather was rather cold.	S.I.
			J. Rawlston... Major	
			for Lt. Col. Comdg. 9th Royal Scots	

Vol 26

154/51

CONFIDENTIAL

WAR DIARY

9TH BATT (HRS) THE ROYAL SCOTS

FROM 1ST APRIL 1917 TO 30TH APRIL

WAR DIARY

Ref. Map: Rœuincourt Trench Map S⁶. MW 1/10,000

or

INTELLIGENCE SUMMARY.

(Erase heading not required.)

9th Bn (N°) The Royal Scots

I

Instructions regarding War Diaries and Intelligence Summaries are contained in F. S. Regs., Part II. and the Staff Manual respectively. Title pages will be prepared in manuscript.

Place	Date	Hour	Summary of Events and Information	Remarks and references to Appendices
ECURIE	1-4-17		The Battalion remained as on 31st inst. - Casualties - Wounded O Cⁿ 6.	S.S.
			Wounded & Killed to date OR 1	S.S.
-do-	2-4-17		The Battalion remained as on 1st Casualty - Killed OR 1	S.S.
MAROEUIL HUTS	3-4-17		The Battalion was relieved by 4th Suffolks &c. and on relief marched to MAROEUIL HUTS.	S.S.
-do-	4-4-17 5-4-17 6-4-17		The Battalion remained at MAROEUIL HUTS.	S.S.
TRENCHES	7-4-17		The Battalion (less reserve personnel left out of action by order of G.H.Q.) moved to the line at 7.30 p.m. C Coy occupying the front line in BONNAL from map 22 to 20 (A 23 c 55.35 to A 23 c 30.85) D Coy the support line (COLLECTEUR) behind and A and B Coys the reserve at ECURIE - Casualties	S.S.
			Killed ... 2 ORs wounded to July. 1 OR. A 30 ft 22 ORs joined	S.S.
-do-	8-4-17		Reserve Personnel and Transport Horses to BRAY. The Batt. Sleyted to ... BONNAL at 10 pm - Casualties. moved to assembly positions in front of BONNAL. Killed 4 ORs wounded 9 ORs	S.S.

[signature]
Lt Col,
Comdg 9th Royal Scots

T.134. Wt. W703-776. 50000. 4/15. Sir J. C. & S.

Army Form C. 2118.

WAR DIARY
or
INTELLIGENCE SUMMARY.
(Erase heading not required.)

Instructions regarding War Diaries and Intelligence
Summaries are contained in F. S. Regs., Part II.
and the Staff Manual respectively. Title pages
will be prepared in manuscript.

Ref. map Rocincourt TRENCH MAP
51 B Nw, 1/10,000

9th B^{ttn.} The Royal Scots
11

Place	Date	Hour	Summary of Events and Information	Remarks and references to Appendices
TRENCHES	9-4-17		The Batt^{n.} had completed the assembly by 3.30 a.m. D Coy being from head of Sap 20 to head of Sap 21 on the right. A Coy from head of Sap 21 to Sap 22 on the left. B Coy in a line behind between Saps 20 and 22 and C Coy in Reserve. Batt^{n.} H^{q.} at head of Avenue G (A23 c. 4.5). The Batt^{n.} were ordered to capture the part of the German line known as the BLACK LINE. The objective and scope of the attack is shewn on 80 N°7—Dated 5th April and is annexed and marked "F". 250 hrs.	
		5.30 a.m.	The barrage opened and the Batt^{n.} attacked and by 7.30 a.m. had captured its objective whilst being obtained with 4th Seaforths. on left and 6th Seaforths. on right. The line was consolidated and carried to the S.A.A. and other Stores to BLUE LINE. Whilst parties opened to S.A.A. and other Stores to BLUE LINE. Whilst parties opened at 9.30 a.m. The attack on the BROWN LINE had been taken at 9.30 a.m. The attack on the BROWN LINE was also successful. Reg^{t.} for Seaforth packet of Seaforths left in BROWN LINE at B14 a and c.	J.J.
	10-4-17		The Batt^{n.} remained in BLACK LINE consolidating.	J.J.

B. Green
Lt. Col.
Comd.g. 9th The Royal Scots

Army Form C. 2118.

WAR DIARY
or
INTELLIGENCE SUMMARY.

(Erase heading not required.)

Instructions regarding War Diaries and Intelligence
Summaries are contained in F. S. Regs., Part II.
and the Staff Manual respectively. Title pages
will be prepared in manuscript.

Ref. Map. ROCLINCOURT TRENCH MAP
5 13 Nov 1 1/10,000

9th Bn. (HTo) Royal Scots.

III

Place	Date	Hour	Summary of Events and Information	Remarks and references to Appendices
TRENCHES	11·4·17		At 9 a.m. the Battalion was ordered to attack the Junction of German strong line between the BROWN LINE at B.14 a and c (see Sketch D attached to Appendix "J") and at 2 p.m. the Batt's were in position in TOMMY TRENCH between points 39 and 69 in following order A B C D - B. HQ at Point 39. The heavy artillery bombarded the part of the BROWN LINE to be taken from the mine. At 5 p.m. artillery bombardment ceased and patrols were sent were pushed out and found that the Germans had evacuated the line. Two Platoons of each Coy were at once ordered forward to occupy its line – line occupied and consolidation started at 5·45 p.m. touch being gained with 7/7 R.61st on the right and 4th London Rif on left. Patrols were pushed out and established own line along railway through B.15 a and at approximately. having been received for the relief of the Batt. by 2nd R.S. 9 (15th Bde 2 in Bn.) and relief commenced about 10 p.m.	13

[signature]
Lt. Col.
Comd 9th Battn. Royal Scots.

T-134. Wt. W708-776. 500,000. 4/15. Sir J. C. & S.

WAR DIARY
or
INTELLIGENCE SUMMARY.

(Erase heading not required.)

Ref map: Rouen & war Trench map 51 B N.W.1 1/10,000

Instructions regarding War Diaries and Intelligence Summaries are contained in F. S. Regs., Part II. and the Staff Manual respectively. Title pages Lens Sheet 11 will be prepared in manuscript.

Place	Date	Hour	Summary of Events and Information	Remarks and references to Appendices
4 Huts, Laressét	12.4.17		Relief was completed at 3.30 am and Battn marched to 4 huts at Laressét.	
			Casualties from 9th to 12th incl:	
			9th: Officers: Killed: 2nd Lt In P Ferguson	
			" " J A W Adams	
			Wounded: Major J Rowbotham MC 8th H.L.I	
			: 2nd Lt Donaldson (died of wounds on 10th.)	
			: A T M Moir	
			: H S Smith	
			: J R Tait 6th R.S off.?	
			: I M MacLennan	
			: G Hutton 3rd R.S	
			: R. C. Brown	
			Wounded at duty: C. J. McLean	
			O.Rs: Killed 69	
			Wounded 138	
			Missing 27	
			B Green	J.9.
			Lt Col	
			Comg 9th Royal Scots	

T.131.   Wt. W708-776.   500,000.   4/15.   Sir J. C. & S.

WAR DIARY

or

INTELLIGENCE SUMMARY.

(Erase heading not required.)

Instructions regarding War Diaries and Intelligence
Summaries are contained in F. S. Regs., Part II. and
the Staff Manual respectively. Title pages
will be prepared in manuscript.

Place	Date	Hour	Summary of Events and Information	Remarks and references to Appendices
LARESSET	12.4.17	10th		
		11th	NIL	
			Wounded 2nd L G Machin (died of wounds 12th)	D.I.
			Officers	
			O.Rs.	
			Killed 2	
			Wounded 2	
	13.4.17		A draft of 5 O.Rs joined for duty on 12th	
	14.4.17	07	The Battalion remained at Y Huts LARESSET	D.I.
LINE	15.4.17		The 51st Division relieves the 9th Division on the battle front from RIVER SCARPE to HYDER- ABAD REDOUBT (H.12.C.1.9.) Exclusive with 152nd Infantry Bde in the front line and 154th Infy Bde in Support. The Battalion left marching via ARRAS - ST NICHOLAS - ST LAURENT FEUCHY - at 2pm and YHUTS at via FICHEUX and bivouacked in H.13 SEAFORD HTRS (26th Infy Bde) about 6pm also band and weapons depots in railway embankment at H.14 a and b. Battalion also in railway embankment at H.13 b.9.2. The 4th Division was in support at H.13 b.9.2. The 4th Division were on the left and 17th Divn on the right. Casualty - Wounded 1 OR	D.I.

b.c.1315/1

(signed) A. L. Col
Comdg 9th The Royal Scots

Army Form C. 2118.

WAR DIARY
or
INTELLIGENCE SUMMARY
(Erase heading not required.)

51B NW Ed6A 1/20000

9th B? (No) The Royal Scots

VI

Instructions regarding War Diaries and Intelligence Summaries are contained in F.S. Regs., Part II. and the Staff Manual respectively. Title pages will be prepared in manuscript.

Place	Date	Hour	Summary of Events and Information	Remarks and references to Appendices
LINE	16.4.17 17.4.17 18.4.17		The Battalion remained as on 15th inst - Casualties on 18th inst - Killed 2 ORs. Wounded - 2nd Lieut. J.E. Hewison (4th R.S. att?.) and 8 ORs. Wounded at duty 2 ORs	S.J.
	19.4.17		Bn and Canad'd Corps remained as on 18th inst. A and B Coys relieved 2 Coys 7th Canados in SUNKEN ROAD in H24 b and d. A.d Hrs in the front line. Reinforcement of 15 ORs joined for duty. Killed 1 OR wounded 2 ORs.	S.J.
	20.4.17		Position as on 19th - After a two hours bombardment of enemy positions in front W of ROEUX about I 19 c 25.30 and hence running in front of MOUNT PLEASANT WOOD at I 19 a 20.15 Coys in SUNKEN ROAD attempted to capture these positions at 8.30pm but being met with strong machine gun fire were unable to do so. Enemy were forced to be occupying French trench running from I.19 a 20.15 to RIVER SCARPE at H24 d 90.65. Casualties - Killed 1 OR, wounded 1 OR.	S.J.

Lt Col
Comdg 9 Royal Scots

T.134. Wt. W708-776. 500000. 4/15. Sir J. C. & S.

WAR DIARY

or

INTELLIGENCE SUMMARY.

(Erase heading not required.)

Army Form C. 2118.

Instructions regarding War Diaries and Intelligence
Summaries are contained in F. S. Regs., Part II.
and the Staff Manual respectively. Title pages
will be prepared in manuscript.

Place	Date	Hour	Summary of Events and Information	Remarks and references to Appendices
LINE	21/4/17	Before dawn	A Coy was withdrawn along SUNKEN ROAD and formed H 24 B 61. From 2 to 3 p.m. our Artillery bombarded the Enemy line running in front of MOUNT PLEASANT WOOD and the Enemy position at the N.E. end of the wood in front of ROEUX. A Coy then attacked these positions getting up to the wood in front of MOUNT PLEASANT WOOD and establishing a post at its junction of this trench and communication trench running S.E. towards ROEUX X WOOD (I.19.A 20.15.) A Coy also got into ROEUX WOOD but were finally forced back to the point on the SUNKEN ROAD they had previously held, owing to heavy machine gun fire and snipers. C and D Coys proceeded to the W. of A and B Coys at 6.30 pm but owing to the uncertain situation only 1 A Coy was distinct, returning to the railway embankment about 2.30 am on 22 nd. The Enemy offered a heavy barrage while C & D Coys were on their way to the line without causing casualties. Sept 16 C.C.7. Casualties Sept 16 Wounded - 2 nd Lt A.F.MATTson (4 th) Killed: CAPTAIN A. TAYLOR and 9 O.Rs R.S. att?) and 31 O.Rs Missing 9 O.Rs	

B. Straun
Lt. Col.
Comdg 9 th 15 th Royal Scots

T.1134.   Wt. W708–776.   500,000,   4/15.   Sir J. C. & 9.

Instructions regarding War Diaries and Intelligence Summaries are contained in F. S. Regs., Part II. and the Staff Manual respectively. Title pages will be prepared in manuscript.

Army Form C. 2118.

WAR DIARY
or
INTELLIGENCE SUMMARY.

(Erase heading not required.)

Ref maps 51 B N.W. Sh.6a 1/20,000

9th Battn. H.Q. The Royal Scots

Place	Date	Hour	Summary of Events and Information	Remarks and references to Appendices
LINE	22.4.17		The position remained as on 21st. The enemy shelled the sunken road occupied by B Coy Coys without doing material damage - most of the rounds use 4.2' and 5.9'. The Battalion was ordered to take part in another attack with the rest of the Brigade and at 6.30 p.m. A Coy left the railway Embankment upon the E side Coy in the SUNKEN ROAD. H.Q. moved to Sunken Road at H 23 B.3.0. 00.03 154 Bde H.Q. Hostile artillery was not so active than on previous days, while our own artillery kept up a ceaseless fire on the enemy positions.	
	23.4.17		The scope and object of the attack and the Battalion and Bde boundaries will be forwarded. 00.78 and instructions for offensive No 771 attacked both along with Map T.S. No M 865, all noted "G". At 4.45 A.m the heavy bombardment opened the enemy putting on his barrage almost immediately in reply. The line of his barrage was the RIVER SCARPÉ - FAMPOUX, the railway bridge over the Ruig in Square H 24 A. At 5.15 A.m the four Coys advanced from the SUNKEN ROAD where	

[signature] Lt Col
Comdg 9th Royal Scots

T.134. Wt. W708—776. 500000. 4/15. Sir J. C. & S.

WAR DIARY
or
INTELLIGENCE SUMMARY.

(Erase heading not required.)

Instructions regarding War Diaries and Intelligence Summaries are contained in F. S. Regs., Part II. and the Staff Manual respectively. Title pages will be prepared in manuscript.

Place	Date	Hour	Summary of Events and Information	Remarks and references to Appendices
	23/4/17		They had formed up in rear of the last wave of the battalions (which they were attached). The Coys on the right (C & D) after going about 150 yds were hung up by heavy machine gun and rifle fire from the right and front. The battalion in front of them were also hung up about the front. The Right Coy (C) pushed into ROEUX WOOD but had eventually to man back their right flank. The Coy next on its left (D) also encountered considerable opposition after going about 150 yards from the second German line running S.W. in rear of MOUNT PLEASANT WOOD. This trench was eventually cleared by a bayonet charge supported by a bomb. This Coy then entered the ... in front of ROEUX. It was found that the sunken road running from I.19.c 8.1 NE towards the village was peopled in strength and further progress was impossible. The two Coys on the left also encountered heavy rifle and machine gun fire from the railway line embankment and the CHEMICAL WORKS after going about 150 yards. a	

[signature]
Lt. Col.
Comd'g 9th Royal Scots

T.131. Wt. W708–776. 500000. 4/15. Sir J. C. & S.

Army Form C. 2118.

Ref No. S I B N W Bd GA 1/20,000

WAR DIARY
or
INTELLIGENCE SUMMARY.
(Erase heading not required.)

X

9th Bn (Scottish) The Royal Scots

Instructions regarding War Diaries and Intelligence
Summaries are contained in F. S. Regs., Part II.
and the Staff Manual respectively. Title pages
will be prepared in manuscript.

Place	Date	Hour	Summary of Events and Information	Remarks and references to Appendices
	23/4/17		number of the Left Coy passed the CHEMICAL WORKS but line was without return apparently having fallen into the hands of the Enemy. The Left and B Coy (A) were also hung up by rifle fire from the direction of CHEMICAL WORKS and from ROEUX and crossroads along the BLACK LINE. Snipers were very troublesome all day both from the flanks and MOUNT PLEASANT WOOD and great difficulty was experienced in locating them and clearing them out. The Enemy artillery fire was very intense and shelled the CHEMICAL WORKS and ROEUX when it was known troops were in those places. Subsequently, the greater part of the SUNKEN RD from ROEUX and the SUNKEN ROAD from Shaft Coy S[?]field. The fire on the Left finally withdrew to the BLACK LINE having been un- able to get any further, and the left being the right of the 51st Division was unable to advance beyond their original front line. These enemy own right flanks, though the +th Gordons Infantry (in Reserve) at one time got past the CHEMICAL WORKS, were brought	

(Signed)
Lt-Col
Comdg 9 R Royal Scots

Army Form C. 2118.

WAR DIARY
or
INTELLIGENCE SUMMARY
(Erase heading not required.)

Instructions regarding War Diaries and Intelligence Summaries are contained in F. S. Regs., Part II. and the Staff Manual respectively. Title pages will be prepared in manuscript.

51 B Nw Suba 1/20,000

Place	Date	Hour	Summary of Events and Information	Remarks and references to Appendices
	23/4/17		which were finally compelled to fall back on the BEACH LINE — In the course we lose by the fighting and the heavy losses sustained by the B.de the 26th NORTHUMBERLAND FUSILIERS (1037? Bde 34th Division) were brought up and took over the right of the line (part of line held by 4th Suffolks) holding the left, and the 4th Norfolks and this Battalion were withdrawn to the Sunken Road from which the attack was launched —	N.9
	24/4/17		At 4.30 a.m. the enemy launched a counter attack opposite the CHEMICAL WORKS which failed and during the rest of the day no attempt to consolidate our communication with the Sunken was main- tained during this Day in spite of occasional breaks but on the 73rd this was impossible owing to the wires being continually broken. Visual signalling was not successful as the smoke from bursting shells obscured the view and the only means of communication was by runner. At 11 p.m. the 197? & the 34th Division were brought up	N.9

Ref map. 51B NW Sh 6A   1/20,000   Title pages Léns Sh. 11.

9th (Sctts) The Royal Scots   Army Form C. 2118.

WAR DIARY
or
INTELLIGENCE SUMMARY.
(Erase heading not required.)

XII

Instructions regarding War Diaries and Intelligence Summaries are contained in F. S. Regs., Part II. and the Staff Manual respectively. Title pages will be prepared in manuscript.

Place	Date	Hour	Summary of Events and Information	Remarks and references to Appendices
LING	24th/4/17		To relieve the Btee, the situation was unchanged from the 23rd.	S.J.
	25/4/17	At 12.50 am.	the Battalion was relieved and marched to ARRAS where it billeted. and at 6.50 p.m. left by train with the remainder of the Bde for LIGNY ST FLOCHEL – The Battn detrained at 10 pm and marched to AVERDOINGT where it billeted (distance about 3 miles). Casualties from 22nd – Killed, CAPTAIN P.A. BLAIR, LT C JAMIESON and 2nd LT J M SUTHERLAND and 54 ORs. Wounded. CAPTAIN G.S.G. STRACHAN, 2nd LT W. CAMPBELL and 2nd LT H.G. BRUNSDON (since of wounds on 24th.) and 115 ORs. Missing, 2nd LT H. COOK (4th Rl. Scots) and 55 ORs.	S.J.
AVERDOINGT	26/4/17		The Battn remained at AVERDOINGT and reorganised. A draft of 27 ORs joined for duty on 27th.	S.J.
– do –	27/4/17		The Battn remained at AVERDOINGT.	S.J.
– do –	28/4/17		The Battn remained at AVERDOINGT – CAPT. J.H. MACDONALD, 7th Royal Scots	S.J.
– do –	29/4/17		and 2nd LT J.S. GELLATLY joined for duty.	S.J.

J Brown
Lt Col
Comdg 9th Royal Scots

Ref Regt LENS Sh 11   9th Bn (Gho) The Royal WbB   Army Form C. 2118.

WAR DIARY

or

INTELLIGENCE SUMMARY.

(Erase heading not required.)

XVII

Instructions regarding War Diaries and Intelligence
Summaries are contained in F. S. Regs., Part II.
and the Staff Manual respectively. Title pages
will be prepared in manuscript.

Place	Date	Hour	Summary of Events and Information	Remarks and references to Appendices
AVERDOINGT	30.4.17		The Battalion remained at AVERDOINGT and commenced Training - a draft of 56 ORs joined for duty. The health of the Battalion for the past month was good and the morale good. For the past three weeks the weather was unseasonable more frequent in general occasions probably the right of the 9th and the weight of the 9th Bn. - the last week was much milder and finer -	S.L.

B. Brown
Lt Col
Comdg 9th Royal WbB

T.134.   Wt. W708-776.   500,000.   4/15.   Sir J. C. & S.

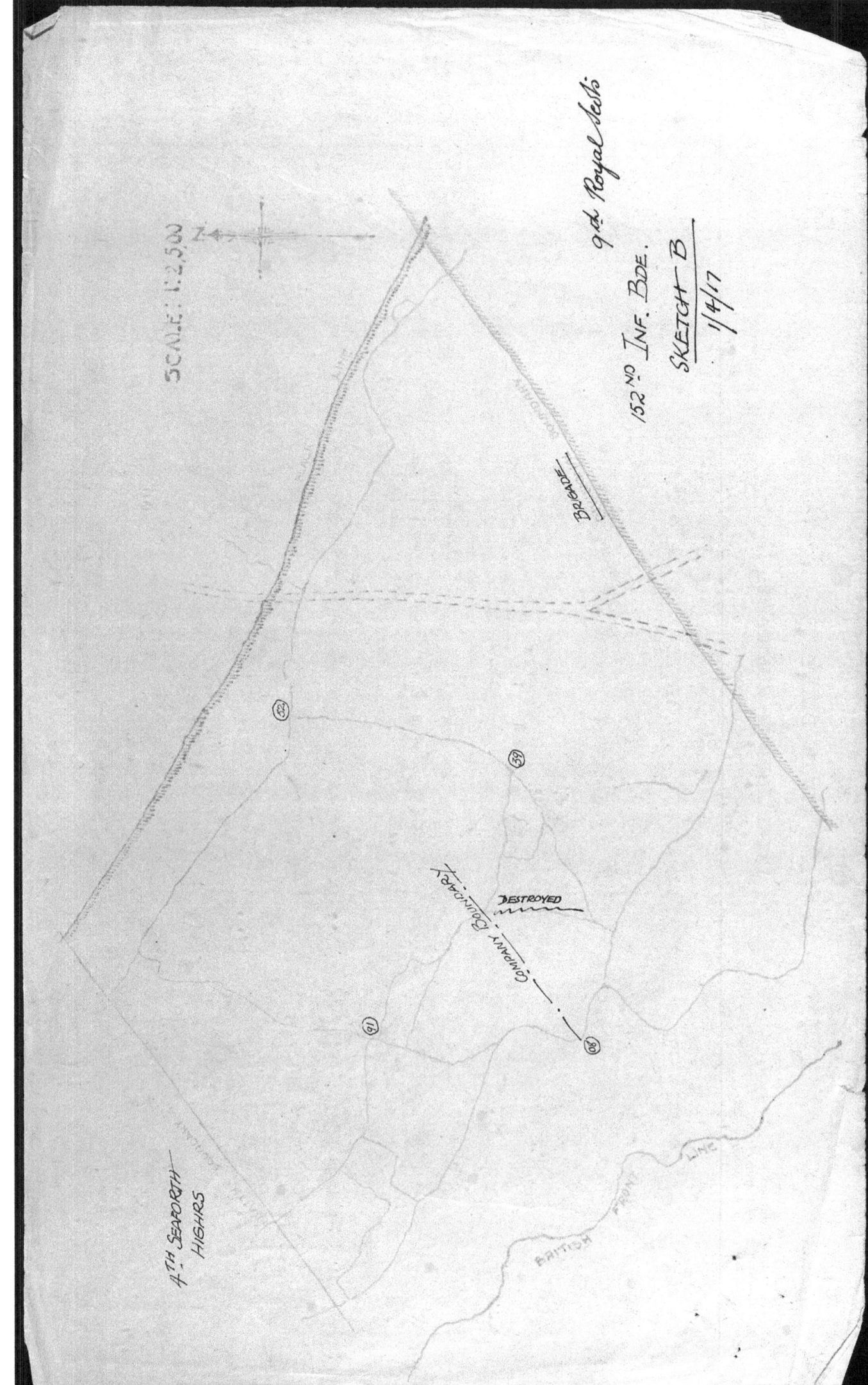

SCALE: 1:2,500

N

9th Royal Scots.

152ND INF. BDE.

SKETCH B
1/4/17

4TH SEAFORTH
HIGHRS

BRIGADE

BOUNDARY

DESTROYED

COMPANY BOUNDARY

BRITISH FRONT LINE

32

39

91

08

SKETCH C

1/4/17

N

Scale 1/20000

SECRET .   OPERATION ORDER No. 70.

                                            Copy No. 7

Reference:- ROCLINCOURT 51B.N.W.1.   5th April 1917.
            Edition 6 A.
        Sketch B, C and D.

I.   GENERAL.   The object of the offensive is to capture
                         the VIMY RIDGE.
                         The Canadian and XVIIth Corps are available
                         for the attack.

II. ORDER OF BATTLE.   Canadian Corps on LEFT with 1st Canadian
                         Division on its RIGHT.
                         XVIIth Corps on RIGHT with 51st Division on
                         its LEFT. 34th Division on its CENTRE,
                                    9th Division on its RIGHT.
                                    4th Division in RESERVE.
                         The 51st Division will attack on a Two Brigade
                         front. The 154th Brigade on the LEFT
                         and 152nd on RIGHT.   One Battalion of
                         153rd Brigade is attached to 154th, and
                         One Battalion to 152nd Inf.Brigades.
                         The 4th Seaforths will be on the LEFT.
                         The 9th Royal Scots on the Right.   The
                         4th Gordons will be in Left Support, and
                         7th A. & S.Hrs RIGHT SUPPORT.

III. OBJECTIVES & BOUNDARIES. The final objective of the Division
                         is to capture MAISON de la COTE to
                         COMMANDANT's HOUSE LINE.   The system
                         will be known as follows :-
                                    BLACK   LINE.
                                    BLUE   LINE.
                                    BROWN   LINE.
                                    GREEN   LINE (Observation Line)
                         These lines are shown on Map.
                         Boundaries between 9th Royal Scots and
                         4th Seaforths and between 9th Royal Scots
                         and 152nd Inf.Brigade are also shown.
                         The OBJECTIVE of 9th Royal Scots and 4th
                         Seaforths will be the BLACK LINE.
                         The objective of the 9th Royal Scots will
                         be the BLACK LINE from A23d95.95 to
                         A23b.05.40.
                         The boundary between Companies will be
                         the line shown on Sketch "B" from
                         A23c93.85 to A23b15.02.

IV. METHOD OF ATTACK.   9th Royal Scots and 4th Seaforths will
                         capture and consolidate BLACK LINE.
                         The 4th Gordon Hrs less two Coys. and
                         7th A.&S.Hrs less two Companies will
                         capture BLUE LINE.
                         Two Coys of 4th Gordons and two Coys of
                         7th A.& S.Hrs supported by two Companies
                         of Battalion of 153rd Inf.Brigade (7th
                         BLACK WATCH) will capture and consolidate
                         the BROWN line.
                         Two Coys of 7th BLACK WATCH are in Reserve.
                         The Leap Frog system will be employed.

V.   @ 9th ROYAL SCOTS. A Coy will be on the LEFT, and D on the
                         RIGHT, B Coy in support, C Coy in RESERVE.
                         A and D Coys will each be on a two platoon
                         frontage, and will attack in two waves.
                         B Coy will attack in one wave. This will
                         form 3rd wave.   The objective of 1st
                         wave is the RED LINE.
                         Objective of 2nd wave YELLOW LINE.
                         Objective of 3rd wave BLACK LINE.

O.C. D Coy will detail one section rifle-men
and one section Bombers from the second
wave to move forward with first wave, and
capture and hold line from A23d.92.80 to
A23d15.70 and C.T. from this line to point
A23d20.88.

First wave will leave Assembly Trench at
Zero plus 2 mins

Second wave will follow at 100 yards interval.

Each wave will consolidate its position
and gain touch with both flanks. Each wave
after having taken its objective must be
prepared to assist next wave if this is in
difficulties. This must not jeopardise the
mopping up.

O.C. B Coy after gaining objective, will
push out Battle Posts as far in front of
BLACK LINE as barrage will allow.

All Commanders having gained their objective
and done the mopping up will re-organise and
post a garrison and be prepared to carry out
further orders. Carrying parties will have
to be found.

VI.   ASSEMBLY POSITIONS.   A Coy will assemble in the 1st ASSEMBLY
Trench from Sap 21 to Sap 22 (this last
inclusive) and touch up with the 4th
SEAFORTHS on LEFT.

D Coy will assemble in 1st ASSEMBLY Trench
from Sap 20 to 21 both inclusive, and touch
up with 152nd Brigade on RIGHT.

B Coy will assemble in 2nd ASSEMBLY Trench
from Sap 20 to 22 both exclusive.

C Coy will assemble Three platoons on left
in 2nd ASSEMBLY Trench, and one platoon on
RIGHT in Third ASSEMBLY Trench.

O.C. C Coy will be at Battn H.Q. in Ave.G.

Completion of ASSEMBLY will be reported by
runner. Time for completion will be given
later.

VII.   ARTILLERY.   The barrage will open at Zero and lift off
RED LINE at Zero plus 4 minutes, and fire
on YELLOW LINE.

It will lift off YELLOW LINE at ZERO plus
7 minutes and move to Intermediate Position
between YELLOW and BLACK Line.

It will lift from INTERMEDIATE POSITION
at Zero plus 10 and move on to BLACK LINE.

It will lift off BLACK LINE at ZERO plus 34
and advance 100 yards from which position
it will lift at Zero plus 38 to a position
100 yards further away from BLACK LINE.

Barrage will remain in this position to
cover consolidation and will not advance
till Zero plus 2 hours and 6 minutes.

VIII.   COMMUNICATION   Communication will be by Runner to H.Q.

O.C.Coys will take with them two H.Q.runners
to bring back first messages.

SIGNALS.

The 1st Canadian Division is using BLUE and
YELLOW flags which will be waved to signify
position.

S.O.S.   which will not come into force
till Flares and V.Pistols are sent up, will
be by Flares only (no rockets). These will
be issued later.

Very Lights

See Addendum 6/7   SoS - Green Succession of
                 Lengthen range - White - do -

Copy N° 7.

TANK SIGNALS. Tank Signals will be as per
Tank,Disc and Light Code as altered.
There will be no Tanks on Divisional
Frontage.

AIRCRAFT SIGNALS. Contact aeroplanes will
fly over the line at Zero plus 1 hour
at Zero plus 3 hours 10 mins.
at Zero plus 8 hours 10 mins.
The most advanced troops should light
flares in the bottom of trenches to indicate
their position.

IX. SYNCHRONISATION OF WATCHES. O.C.Coys will send an Officer to
Battn.H.Q. at 8 p.m. on Y day and at
2 a.m. on Z day. This Officer will
bring two watches.

X. GAS ALERT. Gas Alert will be maintained throughout
the operation.

XI. ASSEMBLY. All troops will be in Assembly positions
by 2-30 a.m. on Z day. This will be
reported to Battle H.Q. by runner.
A Coy will use Sap 21.
D Coy " " Sap 20.
Two platoons of "B")
Two " of "C") will use Sap 22.
One platoon of "B")
One " of "C") will use Sap 21.
One platoon of "B")
One " of "C") will use Sap 20.

XII. Z Day. Z Day is April 8th.
Zero hour will be notified later.

S. Inse
Capt & Adjt.
9th Royal Scots.

Issued at 5. p.m.

Copy No.1 to O.C. A Coy.
" No.2 to O.C. B Coy.
" No.3 to O.C. C Coy.
" No.4 to O.C. D Coy.

Copy No.5 to M.O.
" No.6 to Specialists.
" No.7 to Adjutant.
" No.8 FILE.

SECRET.   REFERENCE OPERATION ORDER NO.70.

                                    5th. April. 1917

          "Z" day is now 9th. April.

                                    S. Inde

                                    Captain & Adjutant.
                                    9th. Royal Scots.

Issued at 10.30 pm

To all recipients of O.O. No.70.

AMENDMENT TO OPERATION ORD R NO.70

Copy No...7.... (ay)

6th. April, 1917

IX.   SYNCHRONISATION OF WATCHES

Delete 7 p.m. and I a.m. and substitute.

8 p.m. and 8 a.m.

Capt. & Adjt.
9th. Royal Scots.

Issued at..1/pm..

To all recipients of O.O. No.70

Addendum to O.O. 70   Copy No 6

7th April 1917.

Para VIII Communications : S.O.S.

Add: S.O.S will be a succession of
Green Very Lights. If the Artillery
are required to lengthen range, a
succession of white Very Lights
will be fired. Range will be
lengthened by increments of
100 yards. These signals came
into force from 12 noon on 7th April
but they are not to be used
during the barrage covering the
assault.

Issued at 10.45 am.   S. Fraser

By 1 O6   A Coy   Captn Adjt
   2   B   9th Royal Scots
   3   C
   4   D
   5   Specialists
   6   Adjt
   7   File

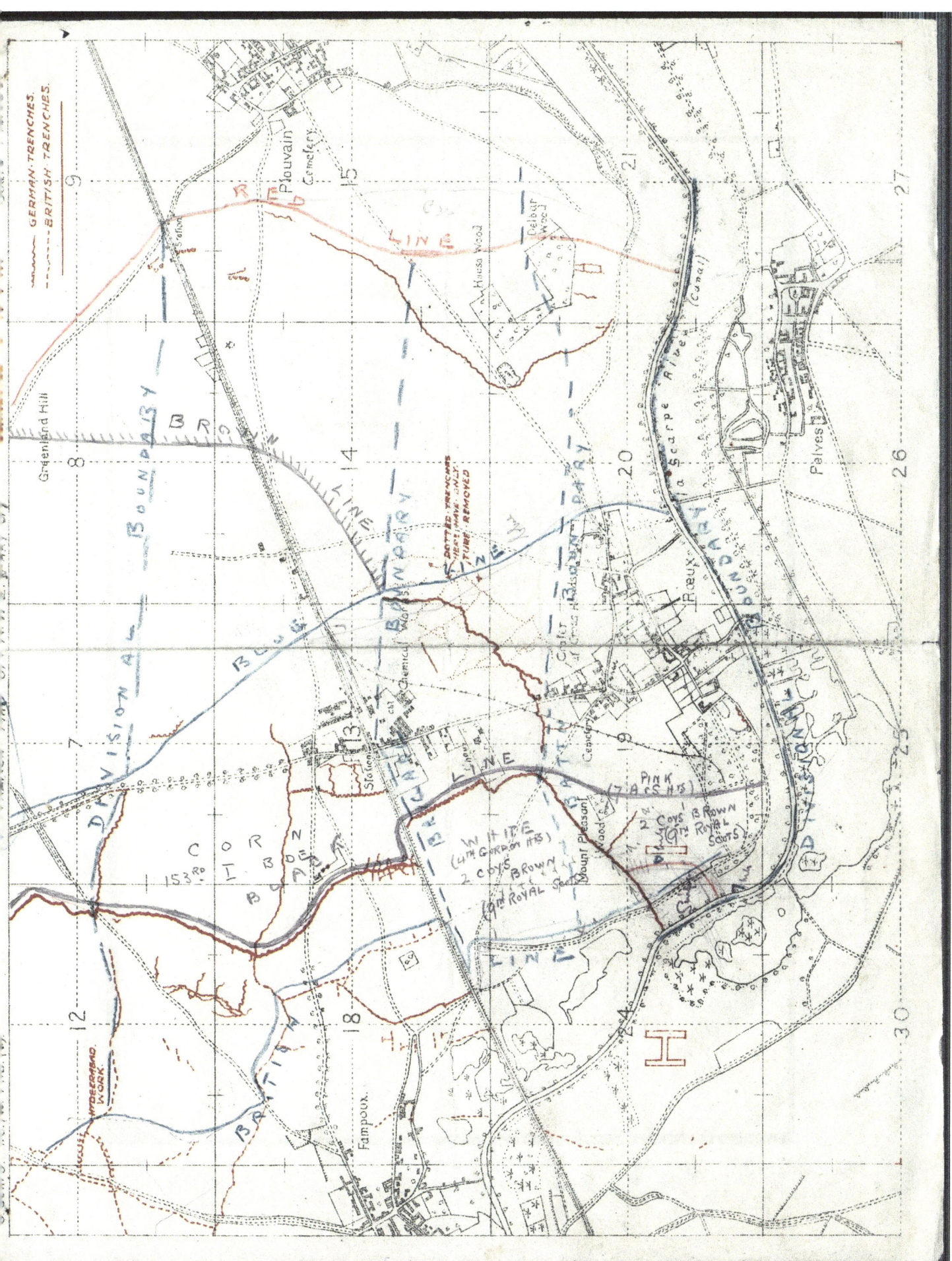

GERMAN TRENCHES.
BRITISH TRENCHES.

RED LINE

Plouvain
Cemetery
Greenland Hill
BROWN LINE
DIVISIONAL BOUNDARY
Hausa Wood
Delbar Wood
Scarpe River (Canal)
Roeux
Pelves

BROWN LINE
BOUNDARY
BLUE LINE

DOTTED TRENCHES
HERE HAVE ONLY
TURF REMOVED

CHEMICAL BOUNDARY

Cot.
CORPS
153RD
GORDON
Station.
BLACK LINE

BRITISH LINE

WHITE
(4TH GORDON H'S)
2 COYS BROWN
(9TH ROYAL SCOTS)
Mount Pleasant
Cemetery

PINK
(7 A'C'S H'S)
2 COYS BROWN
(9TH ROYAL SCOTS)

BRITISH LINE

UNDERGROUND
WORK

Fampoux.

DIVISIONAL BOUNDARY

Secret   aO 78 "G"   Copy 8.

Ry Mafrs.
F/ 3 N.W. Ed 6 A. 1/20,000.
S. No M 8 (6)   22 April 1

1/ Situation as in Instructions issued
2/ Troops taking part in attack.
   Boundaries & objectives as in Instructions.
3 BLUE line will be strongly consolidated
   by 9th R.S. Strong points being
   constructed by B Coy at I 14 c 6, 4.
   and by D Coy at I 20 a. 7. 3.
4 Assembly. 4th Gordons will assemble
   with 2 waves in new trench
   in front of SUNKEN ROAD remaining
   waves in SUNKEN ROAD with A and
   B Coys 7th R.S. attached, A on
   Right B on left, also in SUNKEN
   ROAD. 7th A & S Highrs will assemble
   with their first wave along trench
   running through H 24 d. I 19 c.
   (ie OSMON TRENCH) to trench junction
   I 19 a. 2. 2. thence along trench
   running S.E (ie COLNE TRENCH)
   Remaining waves along SUNKEN ROAD.
   with C and D Coys 9th R.S. attached.
   C on right D on left also in SUNKEN
   ROAD.   9th R.S. will move into
   these positions as soon as it Cos

Ass. 7th A and S Hrs. move into their places of assembly. OC A and B Coys will report to OC 4th G.H. and OC C + D Coys to OC 7th A + S Highrs when in position as well as to Batt HQ OC Coys will see that the whole space covered by the Batt to which they are attached, is covered ~~by the~~

5. BARRAGE will lift from BLUE LINE at ZERO plus 100 -
9th R.S. will advance from SUNKEN ROAD at ZERO + 30 in one wave.

6. Watches OC Coys will synchronise watches with OC Battns to which they are attached at 10 hrs

7. Communications Every use must be made of Visual Signalling for transmission of information

8. O.C. Post Signals cutain left of railway A 23 b. 6.4.

9. The date + hour of Zero is MONDAY 23rd April at 4.45 am
Acknowledge.

S. Ins.
Lieut. Adjt
7th Coyl Scots

Copy 1 OC A
     2   B
     3   C
     4   D
     5   Gordon Hrs.
     6   A + S Hrs
     7   Adjutant
     8   File

<u>No 1</u>   No TT1

Ref Maps   Copy No 6

Sheet 51ᵇ N.W. (Ed 6A) +

Map attached (T.S. M8(6))

1 Enemy are holding GAVRELLE - OPPY LINE to
N of HYDERABAD REDOUBT and to the S.E.
of this point, a newly dug systems which
runs through squares H.12, H.18, I.13,
to west of MOUNT PLEASANT WOOD (I 19c)
    The 1ˢᵗ Army is to advance on
GAVRELLE - OPPY LINE. XVII Corps on left
of Third Army will advance
simultaneously. XVII Corps will attack
with 51ˢᵗ Div on right and 37ᵗ Div
on left.
    17ᵗ Div will advance on right of
51ˢᵗ Div. SOUTH of the SCARPE.
    The objectives of this attack are shown
on the attached map.
    It is the intention to secure the
whole of the high ground on GREENLAND
HILL and SPUR running S.E
through HAUSA and DELBAR Woods.
    Brigade and Battalion boundaries
are shown on attached map.

2   PLAN OF ATTACK
    51ˢᵗ Division will attack with 2
    Brigades
            154 on right
            153 on left

3 battalions. 152 Bde are in reserve.
The final objective of the 154th Bde is
the BLUE LINE

Brigade will attack as follows

7th Argyll & Sutherland Highrs. on RIGHT
supported by C Coy on right and D Coy
on left 9th Royal Scots.

4th Gordon Highrs on LEFT supported
by A Coy on right and B Coy on left
9th Royal Scots

4th Seaforth Hrs in Bde Reserve

7th A & S. Hrs, 4th Gordon Hrs & 9th
Royal Scots will assemble in vicinity
of SUNKEN ROAD through H 24 b & d.

9th Royal Scots Coys in rear of the
Battalions they support, each Coy
in line.

The 7th A & S Hrs. & 4th G H will attack
in 3 waves.

Objective of 1st wave - BLACK LINE
Objective of 2nd wave - Road from
E 19 d 9, 2. to I 13 c 9. 5. 85.
Objective of 3rd Wave - BLUE LINE.

The 9th Royal Scots Companies will
move forward in rear of the last
wave for the BLUE LINE of the
Battalions they support and
consolidate the BLUE LINE

Every man excepting Lewis Gunners
and Bombers carrying buckets

Runners & Signallers, will carry a tool in the proportion of 1 pick to 14 shovels

The consolidation of the BLUE LINE will mean digging a new trench for the most part.

When the last wave of 7th A & S Hrs and 4th G.H leave SUNKEN ROAD 9th Royal Scots will move into it. The assault on the BLUE LINE will take place at ZERO + 100 minutes

~~Consolidation by may will lift from~~
~~BLUE LINE at Zero + 4 hours~~

From ZERO Smoke will be used along SCARPE S of ROEUX

The 153 Bde after the BLUE LINE has been taken will swing northwards from the railway, take the BROWN line and advance to and take the RED LINE.

3/ 1/6 7th A & S Hrs & 4th G.H. will have a combined HQ on the SUNKEN ROAD

9th Royal Scots HQ will be with Bde HQ in SUNKEN ROAD at H 23 b.3.0.

4 The vital importance of accurate reports on the situation is again impressed on OC Coys

4. Reports to be sent in to Hq 1st
A.S. Hrs & 4th London Hrs as well
as to Batt HQ.
5. Tanks will be used to deal with
MOUNT PLEASANT WOOD & buildings
south of Railway and ROEUX

21st April 1917.

S. Inse
Capt. Adjt.
9th Royal Scots

Copy No 1 A Coy
        2 B "
        3 C "
        4 D "
        5 Adjutant
        6 File

CONFIDENTIAL

WAR DIARY ~

9TH BATT. (HRS) THE ROYAL SCOTS

1917

FROM 1ST MAY TO 31ST MAY.

(6202)   W 11186/M1151   350,000   12/16   McA. & W., Ltd.   (Est. 781)   Forms/W 3091/3.   Army Form W. 3091.

Cover for Documents.

Nature of Enclosures.

Notes, or Letters written.

Army Form C. 2118.

WAR DIARY

or

INTELLIGENCE SUMMARY.

(Erase heading not required.)

Instructions regarding War Diaries and Intelligence Summaries are contained in F. S. Regs., Part II. and the Staff Manual respectively. Title pages will be prepared in manuscript.

Place	Date	Hour	Summary of Events and Information	Remarks and references to Appendices
ABERDEEN GT	1-5-17		The Battalion remained at ABERDEEN GT	J.2
-do-	2-5-17		The 15th remained in billets. The following officers joined for duty - 2nd Lts, J.L. GRAHAM, C.S. PATERSON, & J. STEVENSON all 9th R.S. and 2nd Lts W.G. ERRIE, D.WALLACE and J. ALLISON, all 4th Royal Scots.	J.9
- do -	3-5-17		The do remained in billets. A Draft of 14 ORs joined for duty	J.9
- do -	4-5-17		The 15th remained in billets.	J.9
- do -	5-5-17 to 7-5-17		The 15th remained in billets. The following Reinforcement officers joined for duty 7-5-17 - Capt J.T. JOHNSTON, CAPT H. WAKELIN and 2nd Lt. B.A. MORRIS, all 10th Royal Scots	J.9
- do -	8-5-17 to 9-5-17		The Bn remained in billets	
- do -	10-5-17 to 11-5-17		The Bn remained in billets. The following Reinforcement officers joined for duty 10-5-17 - CAPT H. ROSE and 2nd Lts J.B ANNAN, C.A. ROOM and F.B. MOFFAT all 4th Royal Scots and Adjt RC FORRESTER and CAPT N.S. PRINGLE-PATTISON all 7th Royal Scots A Draft of 12 ORs joined for duty	J.9

B. Kern

Lt Col

Comg 9th Royal Scots

Ref: Sheet. LENS Sh. II 1/100,000 FRENCH MAP FRANCE Pt II. Title pages 513 N.W. 1/20,000

9 KB (attd) The Royal Scots   II

WAR DIARY
or INTELLIGENCE SUMMARY.
(Erase heading not required.)

Instructions regarding War Diaries and Intelligence Summaries are contained in F. S. Regs., Part II, and the Staff Manual respectively. Title pages will be prepared in manuscript.

Place	Date	Hour	Summary of Events and Information	Remarks and references to Appendices
Y Huts, bA... RESSET	12.5.17		At 8.30 A.m. the Battalion left AVERDOINGT and marched to Y Huts LARESSET where it arrived at 1.30 p.m. (about 20 kils) Route PENIN, DOFFINE, 12.56 ... HAMEAU - HERMAVILLE - X road 300 yards N.E. of T of LARESSET.	S.9
- do -	13-5-17		The Battn remained at Y Huts	
ARRAS	14.5.17		The Battn marched to ARRAS at 3.10 p.m. arriving at 5.15 p.m. (about 9 kilms) where it went into billets. The Bde are in Reserve, the 57th Divn having taken over the line from 4th Division	S.T. S.9
ARRAS	15.5.17 16.5.17		The Battn remained in ARRAS. Enemy having made strong attack at 3.30 A.m against Divisional front from ROEUX to the CHEMICAL WORKS, Battn received orders at 7.45 Am to move up to camp at H73 a. Bn left ARRAS at 9.30 Am and reached Wilverton at 10.30 Am where it remained until 10.45 pm. The enemy attack was successfully repulled by 152 Inf Bde and Battn moved at 10.45 pm by order of Bde to railway line, Sanctuary at H13 b and also down to Bde trench which took over the portion of the Divisional front from 152 to Bde Bde from the RIVER SCARPE to 13 D 8 2.	S.9

B. Green
Lt. Col.
Comdg 9 Royal Scots

Ref. Map. TRENCH MAP FRANCE 57 ³/N.W. 1/24000

Instructions regarding War Diaries and Intelligence Summaries are contained in F. S. Regs., Part II. and the Staff Manual respectively. Title pages will be prepared in manuscript.

WAR DIARY
or
INTELLIGENCE SUMMARY.
(Erase heading not required.)

Army Form C. 2118.

9th Bn. (Otis) The Royal Scots

III

Place	Date	Hour	Summary of Events and Information	Remarks and references to Appendices
	17-5-17 to 19.5.17		The Battn. remained in Brigade reserve at Railway Embankment. Casualties on 19th. Killed OR 1, Wounded OR 5.	D.J.
	20-5-17		The Battn. left the railway Embankment at 6.30 p.m. and relieved 4th ? ? in Brigade support, railway Embankment at H 24 b 10.00 North 6. A Coy occupying CRATER TRENCH (H 24 b 10.00 North 6) B Coy occupying CRUMP TRENCH (Sunken Road in H 24 B) and C and D Coys occupying Bank north of railway cutting in H 23 c. Battn. HQ in dugout in North side of railway Embankment about H 23 central.	D.J.
	21.5.17		The Battn. remained in support and provided parties for working on forward trenches. Casualties Killed OR 2, Wounded OR 5.	D.J.
	22.5.17		The Battn. remained as on 21st. Casualty wounded OR 1.	D.J.
	23.5.17		The Battn. remained as on 22nd. Casualty wounded OR 2.	D.J.
	24.5.17		The Battn. relieved 4th ? ? in front line held by 3 Coys stewing from North bank of SCARPE about I 26 c.7.7 to I 14 c.15 S. 2 Coy plus one platoon B Coy on right front, C Coy plus one platoon A Coy on left front.	D.J.

B. ?

Lt Col
Comdg 9th Royal Scots

T.131. Wt. W708—776. 50000. 4/15. Sir J. C. & S.

Army Form C. 2118.

WAR DIARY

or

INTELLIGENCE SUMMARY.

(Erase heading not required.)

Instructions regarding War Diaries and Intelligence
Summaries are contained in F. S. Regs., Part II.
and the Staff Manual respectively. Title pages
will be prepared in manuscript.

Ref. Map. TRENCH MAP. FRANCE
57ᶜ N.W. 1/20,000

9ᵗʰ Bn. (Glasgow) The Royal Scots

IV

Place	Date	Hour	Summary of Events and Information	Remarks and references to Appendices
LINE	24·5·17		B Coy (less one platoon) hold one platoon 7A.S.H₂ in right support in trench at West End of ROEUX WOOD (I.19.c.31 to I.19.c.13) and 7A Coy (less one platoon) hold one platoon 7 A.S.H₂ in left support immediately on left of B Coy. 7 A.S.H₂ were in Bde support in position tracked by the R.A.Ks. 153 Bde were on the left and 29ᵗʰ Divison on right on south side of SCARPE. Bde HdQ at I.19.c.8.1 in support. Casualties - Killed O.R. 2. Wounded O.R. 7.	S.9
LINE	25·5·17		CRUMP TRENCH was heavily shelled from 9am to 4pm. C Coy's received a direct hit (map attached). From 4pm till dusk shelling slackened but after midnight the FRONT LINE, ROEUX VILLAGE and CRUMP TRENCH were incessantly shelled with salvoes. Casualties - Killed 4 O.R. Wounded 1 off. (Capt. J.H.McDONALD) 17 O.R. 8 O.R.	H.F.P.
	26·5·17		Very good visibility. Morning quiet except for desultory shelling. In the afternoon CRUMP TRENCH was again shelled and at night the broken trenches were filled between "C" and "B" bridges. Casualties wounded O.R. 8.	H.F.P.
	27·5·17		Enemy's Artillery was concentrated much more on FRONTLINE, SHERIFF POST to SUNKEN ROAD. In the afternoon W.S. Ennis ... Royal W.S.	H.F.P. H.F.P.

T.134. Wt. W708 - 776. 500000. 4/15. Sir J. C. & S.

WAR DIARY
or
INTELLIGENCE SUMMARY
(Erase heading not required.)

Instructions regarding War Diaries and Intelligence
Summaries are contained in F. S. Regs., Part II.
and the Staff Manual respectively. Title Pages
will be prepared in manuscript.

Ref/Map TRENCH MAP. FRANCE
51 B NW 1/20,000

v

Place	Date	Hour	Summary of Events and Information	Remarks and references to Appendices
LINE	27.5.17	(Contd)	was touched in by Shell fire and evacuated. Company HQ in CEYLON TRENCH was blown in. About 10.30 a.m. a small raiding party was sent out to capture a German post but failed owing to Machine Gun fire. Casualties Killed 1 Officer (CAPT. J.T. JOHNSTON) & 1/2 OR 6 Wounded 2 Officers (2.Lt WPSTEEL, & R.C. FORRESTER) & 1/2 OR 8	W.R.
"	28.5.17		Quiet day. At night SHERIFF POST was undug and reoccupied. Relieved by 7th A&SH. and went back to shelters in Railway Embankment at G.13.d. Relief complete about midnight. Casualties - wounded OR 4.	W.R. — W.R.
"	29.5.17		Remained at Embankment. Companies employed in cleaning up and organized into two platoons per company.	W.R.
"	30.6.17		Battalion in shelters in Embankment. Battalion paraded for presentation of cards for gallantry by Commanding Officers. In the afternoon Companies were at shelters of Company Commanders. from GOC Division	W.R.
"	31.5.17		Relieved at Embankment by 8th Black Watch, and proceeded to billets in ARRAS. [signature] Lieut. Col. Cmdg. 9th Royal Scots	W.R.

27 Pl.

Vol 28

WAR DIARY

Notes, or Letters written.

Nature of Enclosures.

Cover for Documents.

9 Battalion (Highlanders) The Royal Scots

From 1 June 1917

To 30th June 1917

(6202) W 11186/M1151 350,000 12/16 McA. & W., Ltd. (Est. 781) Forms/W 3091/3.

Army Form W. 3091.

Ref. maps. ARRAS LENS || HAZEBROUCK.

Army Form C. 2118.

WAR DIARY
or
INTELLIGENCE SUMMARY.

(Erase heading not required.)

1/100,000

9ᵗʰ Bᵗⁿ (Hghs) The Royal Scots.
I.

Instructions regarding War Diaries and Intelligence
Summaries are contained in F. S. Regs., Part II.
and the Staff Manual respectively. Title Pages
will be prepared in manuscript.

Place	Date	Hour	Summary of Events and Information	Remarks and references to Appendices
ARRAS.	1.6.17		Battalion left billets at the CITADEL, ARRAS at 12.15 p.m. and entrained at No 2 station at 2 p.m. Arrived at TINCQUES at 4.30 p.m. The Battalion marched from TINCQUES to VILLERS BRULIN arriving there at 6 p.m. where it billeted.	S.9.
VILLERS-BRULIN	2.6.17		In billets at VILLERS BRULIN. Capt W.M. Urquhart, 2ⁿᵈ Lieut. A. Henderson, 2 Lieut J. Morris joined for duty. Draft of 119 other ranks joined for duty.	S.9.
	3.6.17		In billets at VILLERS BRULIN. Draft of 15 O.R. joined for duty.	S.9.
	4.6.17.		Battalion moved to billets in VALHUON — LE HAMEL. Billets at VILLERS BRULIN were vacated at 6.30 a.m. and battalion reached its destination at 11.10 a.m. having marched via — FREVILLERS — MAGNICOURT — LATHIEULOYE.	S.9.
VALHUON	5.6.17		Battalion left VALHUON at 8 a.m. and marched via TANGRY. — BOIS DE LA BOSSE — BOYAVAL — HEUCHIN to billets in LISBOURG. Arrived in billets at 12.15 p.m. and remained over night.	S.9.

Comdg. 9ᵗʰ Royal Scots. Lieut Col

2449 Wt. W14957/M90 750,000 1/16 J.B.C. & A. Forms/C.2118/12.

Army Form C. 2118.

Ref. Map.

HAZEBROUCK 5A. **WAR DIARY**
&
INTELLIGENCE SUMMARY   9ᵗʰ Bᵗⁿ. (H.S.) 9ʰᵉ Royal Scots.
II

(Erase heading not required.)

Instructions regarding War Diaries and Intelligence
Summaries are contained in F. S. Regs., Part II.
and the Staff Manual respectively.   Title Pages
will be prepared in manuscript.

Place	Date	Hour	Summary of Events and Information	Remarks and references to Appendices
LISBOURG	6.6.17		In billets at LISBOURG.	S.9
NORDAUSQUES	7.6.17		9ʰᵉ battalion moved by busses from LISBOURG to NORDAUSQUES starting at 7.55 a.m.	S.9
			Convoy proceeded via COYECQUE – AVROULT – VIZERNES – Sᵗ OMER – TILQUES, arriving at destination about 11.30 a.m.	S.9
"	8.6.17		In billets at NORDAUSQUES. Battalion commenced programme of training. The following Officers joined for duty :– Capt E.R. REX (6ᵗʰ R.S) 2/Lt L.K. REID, 2/Lt J.C. BANKS, 2/Lt J.K. ALEXANDER (4ᵗʰ R.S) 2/Lt J.M IRVIN (4ᵗʰ R.S) 2/Lt R SMITH (4ᵗʰ R.S) 2/Lt J. WISHART (4ᵗʰ R S)	S.9
"	9.6.17 to 21.6.17		9ʰᵉ Battalion remained in billets and continued training. 9ʰᵉ following reinforcements joined for duty as stated :– 11ᵗʰ – 12 O.Rs 15ᵗʰ – 22 O.Rs 16ᵗʰ – 66 O.Rs 21ᵗʰ – 6 O.Rs	S.9

B.........
Lieut Col.
Comdg. 9ᵗʰ Royal Scots.

2449   Wt. W14957/M90   750,000   1/16   J.B.C. & A.   Forms/C.2118/12.

9th (S) (Tr.) The Royal Scots Army Form C. 2118.

WAR DIARY

or

INTELLIGENCE SUMMARY

(Erase heading not required.)

Instructions regarding War Diaries and Intelligence
Summaries are contained in F. S. Regs., Part II.
and the Staff Manual respectively. Title Pages
will be prepared in manuscript.

Place	Date	Hour	Summary of Events and Information	Remarks and references to Appendices
WULVERDINGHE	22/6/17		The Battalion marched to WULVERDINGHE via MONNECOVE – QUEST MUNT – GOMSPIETTE NORDERBROUCK – WATTEN – LE BERSTACK, leaving NORDAUSQUES at 6.30 am and arrived at 11.Am (distance about 16 kilms) and went into billets	S9
–do–	23/6/17		The Battalion carried on training. A draft of 116 O.R.s joined for duty.	S9
–do–	24/6/17		The Battalion remains in billets – a draft of 48 O.R.s joined for duty.	S9
–do–	25/6/17		The Battalion remain in specks at training by C. Gen. Sir Ivor Maxse K.C.B. XVIII Corps. Major J. Rowbotham rejoined for duty.	S9
–do–	26/6/17		The Battalion remained in billets. A draft of 70 O.R.s joined for duty.	S9
–do–	27–6–17 } 1.9.32		The Battalion remained in billets – carried on training	S.9.
–do–	29/6/17		The Battalion carried on training. A draft of 40 O.R.s joined for July	S.9.

| | | | B. Grieve Lieut Col Comdg 9th Royal Scots | |

2449 Wt. W14957/M90 750,000 1/16 J.B.C. & A. Forms/C.2118/12.

WAR DIARY
or
INTELLIGENCE SUMMARY
(Erase heading not required.)

9th Bn (Nfd) The Royal Sask   Army Form C. 2118.

IV

Instructions regarding War Diaries and Intelligence Summaries are contained in F. S. Regs., Part II. and the Staff Manual respectively. Title Pages will be prepared in manuscript.

Place	Date	Hour	Summary of Events and Information	Remarks and references to Appendices
WULVERDINGHE	30.6.17		The Battalion remained in billets. The health of the Battn during the month was good and the morale good. There is rather too much rain - especially in the first portion of the month and thunderstorms with heavy rain were frequent.	19
			B. Green Lieut Col Comd'g 9th Bn (Nfd) The Royal Sask	

2449   Wt. W14957/M90   750,000   1/16   J.B.C. & A.   Forms/C.2118/12.

28 RS

4429

154/51

not

Notes, or Letters written.

To 31st July 1917.

The Royal Scots

CONFIDENTIAL

WAR DIARY

9th Battalion (Highlanders) The Royal Scots

From 1st July 1917.

Nature of Enclosures.

Cover for Documents.

Army Form W. 3091.

(4497) W. 4884/M680 250,000 8/16 McA. & W. Ltd. (Est. 279) Forms/W 3091/3.

WAR DIARY
or
INTELLIGENCE SUMMARY

(Erase heading not required.)

Instructions regarding War Diaries and Intelligence
Summaries are contained in F. S. Regs., Part II.
and the Staff Manual respectively. Title Pages
will be prepared in manuscript.

Regina HAZEBROUCK 5A.

9th Bn (73rd) The Royal Scots

1/10,000

Trench Map B.S.Corm

28 N.W. 5A.

Place	Date	Hour	Summary of Events and Information	Remarks and references to Appendices
WULVERDINGHE	1·7·17 to 7·7·17		The Battalion remained in billets and continued training	S.I.
– do –	8·7·17		Transport and mounted personnel marched to DERMEZEELE where it billeted for the night	S.I.
D Camp A30 C.14.d	9·7·17		Transport continued march to POPERINGHE and reached Battalion (A.27.d.5.1) and marched to POPERINGHE about 5.45 p.m. Battn. The Battalion left WULVERDINGHE at 1 p.m. entrained in ST OMER (10 Kils) where it entrained and left for POPERINGHE about 5.45 p.m. Battn. detrained at 8.30 p.m. and marched to D Camp. A30 central area. Billeted arrived at 10 p.m. Casualty – wounded OR 1	S.I.
LINE	10·7·17		The Battalion remained at D Camp, until the evening suffering Casualties, killed OR 1, wounded OR 4 from enemy shell fire. At 9 p.m. the Battalion left Camp by Coy to relieve 8th A.B.Bo in the Right sub-sector of the Divisional front. The line taken over Splendid from about C.15.c.5.6 C.14.d.5.7. 39th Division were on the right and 4 Bn Seaforth Hds on the left. The line was held by photo there	S.I.

J. Rowbotham Major
For Commdg 9th Royal Scots

2449 Wt. W14957/M90 750,000 1/16 J.B.C. & A. Forms/C.2118/12.

WAR DIARY
or
INTELLIGENCE SUMMARY
(Erase heading not required.)

Instructions regarding War Diaries and Intelligence Summaries are contained in F. S. Regs., Part II. and the Staff Manual respectively. Title Pages will be prepared in manuscript.

Ref. Ihap. BELGIUM. 28 N.W. S.A.
do - 20F - 2 Ed.

1/9 K.O.Y.L.I. (169) The Royal Scots

$\overline{\text{I}}$

Place	Date	Hour	Summary of Events and Information	Remarks and references to Appendices
LIMA	10.7.17		Platoons of C Coy finding these, the fourth platoon being in reserve at the CANAL BANK (C25a + b); D Coy were in support at THE WILLOWS (C and A and B Coy in reserve at CANAL BANK, with Batn HQ. 3 Camellia B/27	B.9
- do -	11.7.17		The Battalion remained in the line. Enemy's artillery was active in support and rear lines without doing much damage. Casualties — O.Rs 2 wounded, O.Rs 2 wounded at July. O.Rs 2	B.9
- do -	12.7.17		The Battalion was relieved at night by 7 A.S. Hrs and marched back to B Camp; A 30 Central. Enemy again shelled support and rear lines. Casualties — bombers O.Rs 2	B.9
HOUTKERQUE	13.7.17		The Battalion left B Camp at 1 p.m. and marched via POPERINGHE — ST JAN TER BIEZEN — WATOU to HOUTKERQUE (about 15 kils) where it billeted.	B.9
- do	14.7.17 15.7.17		The Battalion remained at HOUTKERQUE. A draft of 20 O.Rs joined for duty on 15'4.	B.9 / B.9

Army Form C. 2118.

WAR DIARY
of
INTELLIGENCE SUMMARY.
(Erase heading not required.)

Instructions regarding War Diaries and Intelligence
Summaries are contained in F. S. Regs., Part II.
and the Staff Manual respectively. Title pages
will be prepared in manuscript.

ST. JULIEN 1/20,000

Ref maps HAZEBROUCK 1/100,000

BELGIUM 28 N.W. 1/20,000

III

9th Bn (T.F.) The Royal Scots

Place	Date	Hour	Summary of Events and Information	Remarks and references to Appendices
HOUTKERQUE	16.7.17 to 21.7.17		The Battalion remained at HOUTKERQUE and continued training — a draft of 15 ORs joined for duty. 20.7.17	a A.J.
WINDMILL CAMP	22.7.17	5.30 AM	The Battalion left HOUTKERQUE at 5.30 AM and marched via WATOU — S'TJAN TER BIEZEN — X country roads to road junction in A.20.d — WORMTSA ROAD to A.16.a — thence military road to WINDMILL CAMP (A.17.d.6.2.) where it went into Bivouac — distance about 16 kilo. — A proportion of the Q.S. personnel remained at HOUTKERQUE. Major W. THORBURN 8th Royal Scots joined for duty.	Q.T. S.S.
— do —	23.7.17 to 29.7.17		The Batt. remained at WINDMILL CAMP	
— do —	30.7.17		The 51st (H) Divn. having, in accordance with the general scheme of attack, been ordered to attack the German Line from C.14.a.4.3 to C.15.a.2.8 as far back as the River STEENBEEK from V.28.d.3.4 to C.5.d.05.15, the Battalion left WINDMILL CAMP at 9.30 p.m. to take up position of assembly on W. side of CANAL BANK at C.25.a.	H

J. Rowbotham
Major
4/ 9th Bn The Royal Scots

Comdg. 9th Bn (T.F.) The Royal Scots

A5834 Wt. W4973 M687 750,000 8/16 D. D. & L. Ltd. Forms/C.2118/13.

Army Form C. 2118.

Ref: Map ST. JULIEN 1/20,000
9th Bn. (H.) The Royal Sco[t]s.

IV

WAR DIARY

or

INTELLIGENCE SUMMARY.

(Erase heading not required.)

Instructions regarding War Diaries and Intelligence
Summaries are contained in F. S. Regs., Part II.
and the Staff Manual respectively. Title pages
will be prepared in manuscript.

Place	Date	Hour	Summary of Events and Information	Remarks and references to Appendices
W: side CANAL BANK C. 25. a.	31-7-17		The Battalion was in position by 12.30 a.m. without casualties. The 152nd & 153rd Bg. Bdes. were attacking on the right and left of the Divisional front respectively. 154th Bg. Bde. was in reserve. The Battalion was in reserve to 152nd Bg. Bde. 38th Division was attacking on the left and 39th Division on the right of 51st (H) Division. 3rd Hour was 3.50 a.m. all objectives were gained by 152nd and 153rd Bg. Bdes. Enemy artillery fire was feeble. Little opposition met with, the enemy freely surrendering. The Battalion remained at CANAL BANK. Killed: Lieut. W. CAMPBELL, M.C. and 16th Rank. Wounded: Lieut. J. S. GELLATLY.	✗

J. Rowbotham
Major
for Lieut. Colonel
Comdg. 9th Bn. (High.) The Royal Scots.

A584 Wt. W4973 M687 750,000 8/16 D. D. & L. Ltd. Forms/C.2118/13.

~ CONFIDENTIAL ~

WAR DIARY.

~ 9th BATTⁿ. (Hrs) ~

~ THE ROYAL SCOTS ~

FROM ~ 1st AUGUST 1917. ~ TO ~ 31st AUGUST 1917.

WAR DIARY

or

INTELLIGENCE SUMMARY.

(Erase heading not required.)

Army Form C. 2118.

Instructions regarding War Diaries and Intelligence Summaries are contained in F. S. Regs., Part II. and the Staff Manual respectively. Title pages will be prepared in manuscript.

STEENEN 1/10,000 1/20,000
BELGIUM 28 July

Place	Date	Hour	Summary of Events and Information	Remarks and references to Appendices
	August 1st		The Battalion remained at Canal Bank till 5.45 p.m. when it proceeded to relieve the 7th Gordon Highlanders in the Front Line & support line of 152 Inf. Bde. Owing to heavy rain the ground was very heavy and relief was reported complete at 12.35 a.m. on 2nd. C. Coy was in right front line (GREEN LINE) from about C.5.d.0.0. to C.5.c.5.5. and D. Coy in left front line from about C.5.c.5.5. to C.5.c.1.9. A Coy was in right support in depth about C.10.4 and B. Coy in left support in depth about C.I.D.4 (BLACK LINE) Old German 2nd line vicinity. 2 Platoons of each of these Coys being permanent garrison and 2 being available for immediate counter attack. Except for the BLACK LINE the Coys being held by Lewis Posts holding from 3 to 8 men. Battalion H.Q. at MINTY'S FARM. (C.10.c.5.1.) Lt. Rayworth was wounded and the Division on right.	J.J.
	August 2nd		Position as on 1st. Enemy heavily shelled front & support positions. After dark working parts were established a East side of Steenbeek to prevent enemy advance. Weather still raining.	
			M. Huntingmajor for Lieut-Colonel, 9th Royal Scots	

A3834 Wt. W4973/M687 730,000 8/16 D. D. & L. Ltd. Forms/C.2118/13.

Instructions regarding War Diaries and Intelligence Summaries are contained in F. S. Regs. Part II. and the Staff Manual respectively. Title pages will be prepared in manuscript.

WAR DIARY
or
INTELLIGENCE SUMMARY.
(Erase heading not required.)

Vol. Bn. (4th) The Royal Berks. Army Form C. 2118.

Place	Date	Hour	Summary of Events and Information	Remarks and references to Appendices
	August 2nd		Enemy continued to shell front and support positions at times heavily. At night Lights were pushed forward to EAST side of SPIENBECK. Weather still windy and raining.	19.
	August 4th.		Position as on 3rd. Enemy artillery fire was not so heavy a continuous as on previous days. Weather rather clearer, and permitted some activity. Battalion was relieved by 1st 9th S.H. Regt. at night and went into Brigade Reserve at CANAL BANK with 3 Companies, 1 Coy occupying the British front line about C.14.d. One prisoner was captured with a patrol just before the relief.	19
	August 5th.		Battalion remained as on right of 4th.	19
	August 6th.		Battalion was relieved by 1st East Yorks (11th Division) and proceeded to entrenchments at Forty Bucket Camp at (A.30 Central). Casualties for period 2nd to 6th - Killed O.R. 15. Wounded Officers ...	19

Major for Lieut Col
Comdg 4th Royal Berks

WAR DIARY

or

INTELLIGENCE SUMMARY.

(Erase heading not required.)

Instructions regarding War Diaries and Intelligence
Summaries are contained in F.S. Regs. Part II.
and the Staff Manual respectively. Title pages
will be prepared in manuscript.

Bd. Ref St Julien 1/40,000.
Belgium 28 N.W. 1/20,000.
Hazebrouck 1/100,000

VII

Place	Date	Hour	Summary of Events and Information	Remarks and references to Appendices
	August 6th (Contd)		2nd Lieut L. K. REID on 3rd and O.R's. 108. Granted gratuity of duty. 2nd Lieuts J. R. BLACK and 2/Lt J. MORRIS on 3rd and O.R. 3. Granting H.	S.9
	August 7th		Battalion remained in camp.	S.9
	August 8th		Battalion moved from camp at 5.A.M. and marched to Tunnelling Camp at St JANS TER BIEZEN arriving about 8.A.M. where Brigade Concentrated. A Strength of 34 offrs Junes for duty.	S.9
	Aug 9th.		The Battn Remained at Tunnelling Camp.	S.9
	do 10th.		The Battn Left Camp at 1.30 p.m. Were in motor lorries to PROVEN where it detrained. It detrained at WATTEN and marched via GANSPETTE - OUEST MONT to BAYEN GHEM Where it went into billets; arriving about 1.45. A strength 1st 117 offrs ranks for duty.	S.9
	11th.		The Battn Remained in billets.	S.9

W. Thorburn
Major for

C. Ing 9th.
Royal Scots

A 3834 Wt. W4973/M687 730,000 8/16 D. D. & L. Ltd. Forms/C.2118/13.

WAR DIARY

or

INTELLIGENCE SUMMARY.

(Erase heading not required.)

Instructions regarding War Diaries and Intelligence Summaries are contained in F. S. Regs., Part II. and the Staff Manual respectively. Title pages will be prepared in manuscript.

Place	Date	Hour	Summary of Events and Information	Remarks and references to Appendices
BAYENGHEM	12.8.17 to 22.8.17		The Battn. remained in billets and carried on training - A draft of 13th and 2nd Lt. R.C. FORRESTER 7th R.S. and a draft of 2 O.Rs joined for duty on 20th. Transport was all mounted personnel left BAYENGHEM at 10 A.M. and marched to TUNNELLING CAMP ST JANSTER BIEZEN, remaining fortnight at WORMHOUDT. q 22nd / 23rd.	1.9.
TUNNELLING CAMP ST JANSTER BIEZEN	23.8.17		The Battn. left billets at 8.15 A.M. and marched to WATTEN WORLIT returned at ST JANSTER at ARQUES and marched to TUNNELLING CAMP, ST JANSTER BIEZEN where it arrived about 1 P.M.	1.9.
- Do -	24.8.17		The Battn. remained in camp. Transport arrived 6 P.M. The following officers joined for duty:- 2nd Lts. G.R. LAWSON, R.J. REID, H.C. LOSSOCK, ITA CHALMERS, G.P. KEPPIE, A.O. GRAY, W.J.K. BONE.	89.
- Do -	25.8.17		The Battn. remained in Camp. 2nd Lt. W. PATON joined for duty.	89.

W. Thorburn Major for Lieut. Col
Commdg. 9th Royal Scots

A.5834   Wt. W4973 M687   750,000   8/16   D. D. & L. Ltd.   Forms/C.2118/13.

9th Bn (HD) The Royal Scots   Army Form C. 2118.

WAR DIARY

or

INTELLIGENCE SUMMARY.

(Erase heading not required.)

BELGIUM Sheet 28 N.W. 1/20,000   1/100,000

V

Place	Date	Hour	Summary of Events and Information	Remarks and references to Appendices
TUNNELLING CAMP ST JANSHOEK BIEZEN	26.6.17 to 28.6.17		The Battalion remained in Camp. A Reinforcement Draft of 17 O.Rs joined for duty.	J.G.
MURAT CAMP	29.6.17		The Battalion marched to MURAT CAMP (B 30 b 3), leaving Tunnelling Camp at 6.10 a.m. Route: via ST JANSTER. BIEZEN — and running about 10.30 a.m. POPERINGHE Road — SWITCH ROAD — VLAMERTINGHE Road — POPERINGHE Road — POTTENHOEK - BRIELEN. Destination reached to Road Junction H 8 B 4 9 — at HOSPITAL FARM B 19 d.	J.G.
"	30.6.17		The Battalion remained at MURAT CAMP. A reinforcement draft of 23 O.Rs joined for duty.	S.J.
"	31.6.17		The Battalion remains in Camp. During the month, the weather was on the whole fine, except the first few days being wet. Casualties by reason of enemy activity three weeks of which took place during the last week to wet cold days. The health was maintained by the Battalion was good.	J.G.

W. Thirburn Major

for Lieut Col Comng 9th Royal Scots

War Diary.

9ᵗʰ Battⁿ (Afri.) The Royal Scots.

—

From – 1ˢᵗ Septʳ 1917

To – 30ᵗʰ Septʳ. 1917.

Instructions regarding War Diaries and Intelligence Summaries are contained in F. S. Regs., Part II. and the Staff Manual respectively. Title pages will be prepared in manuscript.

Army Form C. 2118.

Ref map 'BELGIUM' Sh. 28 NW I/20,000
POELCAPPELLE Ed 1-1/10,000

9th Bn (T.F.) The Royal Scots

WAR DIARY
or
INTELLIGENCE SUMMARY.

(*Erase heading not required.*)

Place	Date	Hour	Summary of Events and Information	Remarks and references to Appendices
MURAT CAMP	1-9-17 to 3-9-17		The Battn remained at MURAT CAMP	R.S.
DIRTY BUCKET CAMP	4-9-17		The Battn moved to DIRTY BUCKET CAMP (A30 Central) owing to hostile shelling of MURAT CAMP	S.S.
- do -	5-9-17		The Battn remained in Camp.	S.S.
LINE	6-9-17		The Bttn relieved the 152nd Bde. in the line - the Battalion (less Echelon B) relieved 8 A.I. Bn in the right subsector of Divisional front leaving DIRTY BUCKET CAMP at 3.15 pm. A Coy was in right front. B Coy in left front. C Coy in support at MON DU RASTA (C5 A 7.1) and D Coy were in reserve in echelon behind in front of STEEN BEEK - D Coy was in reserve at MURAT CAMP. The line linked over van from VIEILLES MAISONS (C6 B 3.2) to on the right to the LEKKER BOTERBEEK at U 30 C. 6. 7 and consisted of posts. The dividing line between C coy being just in front of BULOW FARM (U30 C 8.1) - 3 platoons of each Coy were in the front posts with 1 platoon of each in immediate support about C6 A 3.5. Battn HQ was at MON BOEGAES (C5 C 8.8). MURAT CAMP ...	

O.C. 9th Royal Scots

A5834   Wt. W4973 M687   750,000   8/16   D. D. & L. Ltd.   Forms/C.2118/13.

Ref. Map POELCAPPELLE Edn. 1/10,000
BELGIUM. 28.IV.16. 1/20,000

Instructions regarding War Diaries and Intelligence
Summaries are contained in F.S. Regs. Part II.
and the Staff Manual respectively. Title pages
will be prepared in manuscript.

Place	Date	Hour	Summary of Events and Information	Remarks and references to Appendices
Lijne	6.9.17		Enemy in the Evening - Casualties 4th Seaforth Attd here on his left and 2/8th London Regt. (58th Divn) on the Right. 7th A & S Hrs to be in Reserve to Battn at YSER CANAL BANK, 4th GORDON Hrs being in Reserve 4th Seaforth Hrs - CASUALTIES. WOUNDED ORs 6 - Wounded at July ORs 2.	L.J.
- Do -	7.9.17		The Battn remained in the line - D Coy moved to DUETERGOULF CANAL BANK.	L.J.
- Do -	8.9.17		The Battn remained in the line - Casualties KILLED - ORs WOUNDED at July ORs o - o - R Coy moved to VON WERDER'S HOUSE (C.10.B) (NCOs and 1 platoon) KNIGHT FARM (C.11.B - 2 platoons and 2 platoons) AUSTERLITZ FM (C.5.c - 2 platoons). Casualties KILLED ORs 7. Wounded ORs 10. Wounded at July ORs 4.	L.J.
Canal Bank	9.9.17		The Battn was relieved by 7th A & S Hrs in the Evening and went into Isle. Isane at CANAL BANK. Casualties: Wounded at July ORs 2.	L.J.
- Do -	10.9.17		The Battn remained at CANAL BANK - Casualties - Wounded at July ORs 2. CHALMERS and ORs 2.	L.J.
- Do -	11.9.17		The Battn remained at CANAL BANK.	L.J.
SIEGE CAMP	12.9.17		The Battn was relieved by 7th GORDON Hrs (153rd Bde) and marched to SIEGE CAMP (C2: IC) and went into Divisional Reserve - Casualties - Wounded 2nd Lt J WISHART (4th R S attd) and 2nd Lt H.C. LOSSOCK.	L.J.

signature
Comdg 9th Royal Scots

A5834 Wt. W4973/M687 750,000 8/16 D.D. & L. Ltd. Forms/C.2118/13.

Army Form C. 2118.

WAR DIARY
or
INTELLIGENCE SUMMARY.
(Erase heading not required.)

Instructions regarding War Diaries and Intelligence
Summaries are contained in F. S. Regs. Part II.
and the Staff Manual respectively. Title pages
will be prepared in manuscript.

9th Bn (H) The Royal Scots

Ref Map. BELGIUM : 28 N.W. /20.0.00
POELCAPPELLE 1/10,000 -

III

Place	Date	Hour	Summary of Events and Information	Remarks and references to Appendices
SIEGE CAMP	13.9.17 to 18.9.17		The Battalion Remained at SIEGE CAMP and carried on with training.	S.J.
LINE	19.9.17		Relieved "B" Bns to HOUTKERQUE at 10.30 a.m under Command of CAPT A.D. MAXWELL. The Remainder of the Battalion moved at 8.30 from to the line & late in assembly position preparing to assaulting the enemy's defences. Casualties wound 2nd Lt D.R. FORSTER 4th R.S. att? and 70 o.r.'s wounded at Duty Capt. W.M. UR QUHART.	S.J.
- do -	20.9.17		Assault was completed by 5.35 a.m and was made difficult by heavy rain which fell about midnight 19/20th. Instructions for the advance with relative maps are attached - the front to be attacked by the Battalion extended from the junction of LANGEBOEK BEEK and PHEASANT TRENCH (U 30 d 2 9) to junction of PHEASANT TRENCH and tub tram to FLORA COTT (C 6 B 90 15). 250 dump was S.40th at which hour the barrage opened and the men got well away close up to the barrage. PHEASANT TRENCH on the right between C 6 B 30 B and U 30 d 45, which by 6.45 a.m was all cleared of any hands was captured and consolidated. S.J.	

WAR DIARY
or
INTELLIGENCE SUMMARY.
(Erase heading not required.)

Rfthng POELCAPPELLE Worrism   9th Bn (50) The Royal 50th   Army Form C. 2118.

IV

Place	Date	Hour	Summary of Events and Information	Remarks and references to Appendices
	20.9.17		Considerable opposition from strong points about C.6.B.6.3 who opened fire — Bomb who kept with Batte on right (2/8th London Regt) thronghout from the start. On the left from POELCAPPELLE ROAD to LEKKER-BOTERBEEK till attacking through B Coy who stopped by heavy machine fire and retired to our lines. Here they were quickly reorganised by Lt F.M. SCOTT (O.C. B Coy) with the assistance of 2ndLt. J.R. BLACK (the Battalion Intelligence officer) and an artillery liaison officer and again advanced and captured the trench, being assisted very greatly by the action of the section commander on the right flank of the Company Who, surprising the Enemy still holding the trench to his left, worked along it. It seems unwise (Camnd Coy) passed through trenches the STRONMBEEK with very slight opposition. Reached on the Rhann right of C Coy who they came in on flanks rifle fire from HUBNER FARM which was strongly held. And came forward to C.9.10 and came forward on this point to support the advance of 2/8th LONDON REGT. Afterwards fully captured this point, after which Hubner was finally captured and an important point. Right Coy (D) (C) Shittelgut a point	

Comdg 9th Royal 50th

Lieut Col

A.5834 Wt. W.4973 M687 750,000 8/16 D. D. & L. Ltd. Forms/C.2118/13.

Army Form C. 2118.

WAR DIARY
or
INTELLIGENCE SUMMARY.

(Erase heading not required.)

Instructions regarding War Diaries and Intelligence
Summaries are contained in F. S. Regs., Part II.
and the Staff Manual respectively. Title pages
will be prepared in manuscript.

Ref map. POELCAPPELLE 1/10000

9th Bn (H) the Royal Scots

Place	Date	Hour	Summary of Events and Information	Remarks and references to Appendices
HNE	20·9·17		at D.1.A.6.2 Whose party from 7/8th LONDON REGT was met. The Battalion was established on the line of the STROOMBEEK by 8.10.am. The Companies on the left (D Coy) having suffered considerable losses in reaching and in the vicinity of PHEASANT TRENCH – the 7 K.A.B. They were well up to the leading wave at the STROOMBEEK in artillery formation and advanced through in good time to catch up their barrage. The advance of the Sherwoods & the 3/Staffs until well on in the afternoon was uneventful – The Enemy put down heavy barrages with great intensity on the line of the ST JULIEN – LANGEMARCK road along the day, but damage gained about 6 minutes after 3.30. He also shelled our positions at odd times. After a heavy counterattack the Enemy counterattacked at 6 p.m., but in sight of the attack by advanced against the Brigade left. The Battalion (4 Regonth Ho) on our left returned to PHEASANT TRENCH, the Battalion infantry them (4 platoon Ho) having been driven back. The left Flank of 7.07.7 Ho having been placed debro Sur movement from D Coy to assist them, and at the same time to Companies (B Cos) in	

A5834 Wt. W4973 M687 750,000 8/16 D. D. & L. Ltd. Forms/C.2118/13.

B Trevor
Cmmdg 9th Royal Scots

WAR DIARY
or
INTELLIGENCE SUMMARY.
(Erase heading not required.)

Instructions regarding War Diaries and Intelligence Summaries are contained in F. S. Regs., Part II. and the Staff Manual respectively. Title pages will be prepared in manuscript.

Place	Date	Hour	Summary of Events and Information	Remarks and references to Appendices
LINE	20.9.17		PHEASANT TRENCH formed a reference flank to the left. Casualties were inflicted on the enemy from our posts about the junction of ZEVKOER BOTERBEEK and STROOM BEEK whenever able to enfilade the enemy when advancing. At 6.5 pm the Battalion on our left were re-pulsed moving forward again and position appears satisfactory when darkness set in.	
-do-	21.9.17		At midnight 20/21 a message from the R.S.F. on our left was received stating that the line held by the front Battalion on left (at Suiton St) was WHITE HOUSE – PHEASANT FARM 16 U 30 b 9.2 with posts in front – "D" Coy were ordered to hold forward between 7A St Mho (which had thrown back their left flank) and the Battalion on the left – this by photo along line of ZEVKOER BOTER BEEK between the STROOMBEEK and POTSH CAPPELLE ROAD – so it was now in the front line – One platoon from Right support Coy ("A" Coy) was sent to D Coy as reinforcement. At 2pm at the request of 7A St Mho one platoon from Right front Coy ("C" Coy) was sent forward to the S.W. final their Reserve Coy. Kept in with mutual silling and occasional forward reps. the two companies maintained	

Instructions regarding War Diaries and Intelligence
Summaries are contained in F. S. Regs., Part II.
and the Staff Manual respectively. Title pages
will be prepared in manuscript.

WAR DIARY

or

INTELLIGENCE SUMMARY.

(Erase heading not required.)

Ref. Map: POELCAPPELLE 1/20000

9th Bn: (Hts) The Royal Scots

VII

Place	Date	Hour	Summary of Events and Information	Remarks and references to Appendices
LINE	31-7-17		fully and the Situation remained unchanged until 6.30 p.m. when the enemy again counter attacked along the whole front. This attack was anticipated and heavy shell and some rifle and machine gun fire. The remnants of the right were quiet and the Battalion was relieved by 6th SEAFORTH H'RS and 6th GORDON H'RS (152 & 9 Inf Bde) and marched back to SIEGE CAMP. During the operations about 100 prisoners were captured and 8 machine guns and one light Trench mortar were taken. Communication by telephone was found impossible owing to the wires continually being broken and the most reliable means of communication were ④ runners who got through enormously well specially two 625 p/pairs which were invaluable.	
			Casualties on 30th – 31/7/17. Killed : 2nd Lt C J McLEAN, 2nd Lt J ALLISON 4th R.S. attached, 2nd Lt J.K. ALEXANDER 4th R.S. Wounded: 2nd Lt J M IRVIN 4th R S att. and 2nd Lt. R.P. FK SER – Casualties O.R.20/31 – Killed - O.Ra 31 Wounded O.Ra 155 wounded at attk. O.Ra 8 missing O.Ra 27	
				J.J. [signature] Lieut Col Comdg 9th Royal Scots

Ref Map BELGIUM 28 NW 1/20,000 1/10,000
HAZEBROUCK LENS 1/100,000

WAR DIARY
or
INTELLIGENCE SUMMARY.

Army Form C. 2118.

(Erase heading not required.)

Instructions regarding War Diaries and Intelligence Summaries are contained in F. S. Regs., Part II. and the Staff Manual respectively. Title pages will be prepared in manuscript.

VIII

Place	Date	Hour	Summary of Events and Information	Remarks and references to Appendices
SIEGE CAMP	22.9.17 to 23.9.17		The Battalion Remained at SIEGE CAMP D and Reorganised. During am. Coys were active and bombed camp - Casualty on 22nd - wounded 1 OR.	N.1
POPERINGHE	24.9.17		The Battalion left Camp at 3.20 pm and marches to POPERINGHE (8 kils) where it went into billets.	N.2
-do-	25.9.17 to 28.9.17		The Battalion remains in billets until 11.15 pm when it marches to HOPOUTRE. Train left at 3.30 pm and arrives at BAPAUME - Train left for BAPAUME - BAPAUME at 12.40 am 29th.	N.3
COURCELLES	29.9.17		The Battalion Detrained at BAPAUME and marched via BIHUCOURT and ACHIET LE GRAND to COURCELLES where it went into billets.	N.3
-do-	30.9.17		The Battn remained in billets. During the month the weather was dry and Sunny - The health and morale of the Battalion were good.	N.3

B...
Lieut-Col
Comdg 9th S Bn. The Royal Scots

Copy No.10.
16th September 1917.

APPENDIX I
to Instructions for Offensive Operations I 2.
- - - - - - - - - - - - - - -

COMMUNICATION. Runners. 4 Runners per Company will go with Bn. H.Q.

Wireless Station will be established at ~~XX. XXXXX~~ RED HOUSE

Power Buzzer. Two allotted to Battalion - one at BULOW FARM. The other will be established at NEW HOUSES as soon as DOTTED BLUE LINE is taken.

Pigeons. 2 Pigeons will be allotted to each Company. A map is printed on back of pigeon message forms. This map will be carried to Divisional Headquarters: only written parts of message being telegraphed to addressee. Map references must therefore be given as well as marking positions on Map. Messages will be addressed to Bn. Hq. Pigeons must be released as follows:-
    "A" Coy from PHEASANT TRENCH as soon as PHEASANT TRENCH on right is captured.
    "B" Coy from PHEASANT TRENCH as soon as PHEASANT TRENCH on left and NEW HOUSES are captured.
    "C" Coy from FLORA COTT. when it is captured.

Rockets. 2 Message carrying rocket will be issued to each Company. Range of Rockets is 1000 yards.

Visual. Brigade Station will be established at PHEASANT FARM which will work to Battalion Headquarters and if weather is clear to CANE POST. Every endeavour will be made to establish visual stations consistent with safety, advantage being taken of lateral communications if direct communication cannot be obtained.

Telephone. Communication will be established by telephone, if possible, as follows:-
    Bn Hq to NEW HOUSES laid and maintained by Bn Hq.
    Bn. Hq to "B" Coy H.Q. by T in on ex NEW HOUSES line.
    NEW HOUSES to "D" Coy H. Q. laid and maintained by D Coy.
    Bn. Hq to A Coy H.Q. laid by Bn H.Q. and maintained by A Coy.
    A. Coy H.Q. to C. Coy H. Q. laid by A Coy and maintained by C Coy.

General. (i) On Z day messages by Power Buzzer will be sent in clear.

                    (ii) Code Calls of Signal Stations will be as follows:-

Bde H. Q.	L. A.
FERDINAND FARM.	U. D.
RAT HOUSE.	V. B.
BULOW FARM.	W. B.
PHEASANT FARM.	Y. C.
NEW HOUSES.	Y. D.
A. Coy.	A. R.
B. "	B. R.
C. "	C. R.
D. "	D. R.
4th Gordons Adv Post.	G. F.
7th A. & S. Hrs. Do	A. F.

(iii) S. O. S. (a) Grenade bursting into 2 red and 2 green flares.

(b) 2 red and 2 green Very lights fired in quick succession in that order.

S. Fraser

Acknowledge.

Capt. & Adjt.
9th Royal Scots.

DISTRIBUTION.

Copy No 1 to O.C. A Coy.
" 2 " B "
" 3 " C "
" 4 " D "
" 5 Signalling Sergeant.
" 6 C.O.
" 7 Adjutant.
" 8 8th Post Office Rifles.
" 9 War Diary.
" 10. Do.

DISTRIBUTION.

```
Copy  No 1  to O.C. "A" Coy.
 "    No 2  to  "   "B" "
 "       3      "   "C" "
 "       4      "   "D" "
 "       5      Signal Sergeant.
 "       6      C.O.
 "       7      Adjutant.
 "       8      8th Post Office Rifles.
 "       9      War Diary.
 "      10          Do.
```

WAR DIARY

Instructions for Offensive Operations I 2.

REFERENCE MAPS. POELCAPPELLE Ed. 3. 1/10,000.
Map "A" attached.

GENERAL. 1. On a date and hour to be notified later
(Z day and Zero hour) XVIII Corps will
resume the attack on the German defences
N.E. of YPRES.
XVIII Corps attacks with
51st (H) Division on Right.
20th Division on Left.

51st (H) Division attacks with 154 Inf.
Bde.

The 154 Inf. Bde. attacks with
9th Royal Scots on Right and
4th Seaforth Highlanders on left - to
first objectives, followed by
7th A. & S. H. on right and
4th Gordon Hrs on left - to final
objectives.
8th Post Office Rifles.
1/5 L.R.B. will attack on right of 9th
Royal Scots, followed by *2/5 LRB*

OBJECTIVES AND BOUNDARIES.

2. Objectives and boundaries of Brigade
and Battalions as on POELCAPPELLE Map -
and of Companies on Map A.

(1) OBJECTIVES OF DIVISION.
First objective - Dotted Blue Line.
Final objective - Blue Line.

(II) OBJECTIVES OF BATTALION.
First objective - Black line.
Final objective - Dotted Blue Line.

(III) BRIGADE AND BATTALION RIGHT BOUNDARY.
C 6 B 35.05 - C 6 B 20 15 - D 1 a 65.20 -
D 2 a 00.25 (the FLORA COTT - WINCHESTER
ROAD inclusive)

(IV) BATTALION LEFT BOUNDARY.
LEKKERBOTERBEEK.

(V) INTER COMPANY BOUNDARY.
C 6 B 00 65 - C 6 B 20.75 - U. 30.D 80.20
-ROAD to BAVAROISE HO. (inclusive to C Coy.

3. PLAN OF ATTACK.

    (I) 9th Royal Scots on right and 4th Seaforth Hrs
    on left will capture, mop up and consolidate
    the ground up to Blue Dotted Line, and also make
    good the ground up to the protective barrage in
    front of Blue Dotted Line

    (II) The Battalion will attack with "A" and "B" Companies
    in front. "A" on right, "B" on left - Objective Black
    Line (Map A) followed by "C" and "D" Companies - "C" on
    right, "D" on left = Objective Dotted Blue Line (Map A)
    "A" Company's objective includes:-

Point	A	C.6. B.7.3.
"	B	C.6. b.6.3½.
"	C	C.6. b.7½.2.
"	D	C.6. b.8.4.
"	E	C.6. b.9.6.
"	F	U.30.d.6½ 1.
"	G	U.30.d.8. 9.
"	H	U.30.d.8½.0.

"B" Company's objective includes:=

Point	I	U.30.d. 9. 3. -
"	J	U.30.d. 4½.2½.
"	K	U.30.d. 3½.3½.
"	L	U.30.d. 4. 4.
"	M	U.30.d. 3. 5.
"	N	U.30.d. 3. 6.
"	O	U.30.d. 2. 7.
"	P	U.30.d. 2. 8½.

"C" Company's objective includes:-

FLORA COTT. (	Point Q	D. 1. a 2.	3½.
(	Point R	D. 1. a 2½.	4½.
	Point S	D. 1. a 4.	4.
	Point T	D. 1. a 6.	2.
	Point U	D. 1. a 4.	6.
	Point V	V. 25 c 1.	1.

"D" Company's objective includes:=

NEW HOUSES	U. 30.d.6.	3.
Point W	U. 30.d.8.	2½.
" X	U. 30.d.7.	3¼
" Y	U. 30.d.6.	8.
" Z	U. 30.d.5.	9.
" X2	V. 25.c.2.	4.
" Y2	U. 30.d.9.	7.

    These points will be consolidated and held
as strong points.

    O.C. "C" and "D" Companies will patrol forward to
make good the ground between the STROOMBEEK (Dotted
Blue Line) and Protective Barrage, to enable 7th
A. & S. H. to form up beyond STROOMBEEK.

    (III) Companies will be formed up as shown on Map A.
A tape will be laid to show first line.
    Leading waves will advance at Zero. There will
be 10 to 15 yards between ranks: 25 to 30 yards
between waves.

(IV)   "A" Company will establish its Headquarters at Point
"B", "B" Company at Point "J", "C" Company at FLORA COTT.
(Point "R.")   and "D" Company at Point "X."

(V)   On reaching objectives Companies will consolidate
by lines of posts in depth.
Immediately Companies have taken their objectives
and consolidated, O. C. Companies will re-organise
one Platoon per Company for immediate counter-attack
in the event of their line being penetrated at any
point.   When Blue Line has been taken and consoli-
-dated "A" and "B" Companies will be prepared to move
forward to immediate Counter-attack in the event of
the Blue Line being broken. O. C. these Companies
will move forward to attack on their own initiative
should they see the enemy have broken through, but
O. C. "A" Company must assure that his right flank is
secure before taking men away from that point.
O. C. "A" and "C" Companies will be prepared to form a
defensive line to their right in the event of the
Battalion on our right being held up.
The main line of resistance will be the line
DELTA HUTS - PHEASANT FARM - PT. 68 - FLORA COTT.
and will be held at all costs.
These Companies will also be available to form
forward dumps.

(VI)   O. C. "C" Company will detail a party of 1 N.C.O
and 2 men to shake hands with a party from 8th Bn office rifles
1/5 L.R.B. at ROAD JUNCTION D 1 a 6. 2.

           O. C. "D" Company will detail a party of 1 N.C.O
and 2 men to shake hands with a party from
4th Seaforth Highlanders at junction of LEKKERBOTERBEEK
WITH POELCAPPELLE -ST JULIEN ROAD.

4. **HEADQUARTERS.**
       154 Infantry Brigade CANE POST C. 9. a. 6. 3.
       Advanced Report Centre) FERDINAND FARM
       154 Infantry Brigade.) C. 5. c. 0. 5.
       9th Royal Scots.   BULOW FARM U. 30. c. 9. 2.
       7th A. & S. Hrs.   Do   Do   -   Do
       4th Seaforth Hrs.   DOG HOUSES U. 29. b. 7. 4.
       4th Gordon Hrs.   U. 29. d. 82. 58.

5. **MACHINE GUNS.**
       When it is known that the Dotted Blue Line is
taken, two guns of 154 M. G. Coy will go forward to
FLORA COTT. Vicinity of V.25. c. 1. 2.

6. **TRENCH MORTARS.**
       Two Stokes Guns are allotted to 9th Royal Scots
and will be used as an initial barrage against enemy
post at VIEILLES MAISONS. They will remain at VIEILLES
MAISONS until they receive further orders

7. **ARTILLERY.** The attack will be preceded by a 24 hours intense bombardment, the 152 and 153 T.M. Batteries co-operating. The barrage will be put down 150 yards in front of the forming up position - It will lift at Zero plus 3 minutes and move in 50 yards lifts -For the first 200 yards the barrage will move at the-rate of 50 yards every two minutes. After the first 200 yards,-at 50 yards every three minutes up to the Dotted Blue Line: From Dotted Blue Line to Blue Line at 50 yards every four minutes. Details of lifts and pauses with barrage map will be issued. In addition to Artillery barrage there will be a Machine Gun Barrage.

8. **TANKS.** Two Tanks will assist in the capture of NEW HOUSES, and two in the capture of FLORA COTT., but their arrival must not be waited for and Companies must push on without them should they not appear. Tanks will come from the direction of ST JULIEN moving along POELCAPPELLE ROAD. They will afterwards move forward to Blue Line.

<u>SIGNALS</u> between Tanks and Infantry
RED.)
WHITE.) Disc - Enemy in Concrete emplacement.
RED.)
RED DISC. Position captured
RED.)
RED.) Disc - Tank broken down.
RED.)

If the help of a Tank is required men will signal by waving steel helmets on top of rifles.
The position of Tanks will be marked on Maps as under:n

                  Tank in action.

                  Tank out of action.

Whenever possible, when marking Tanks on Maps the Battalion Letter and Number will be stated. The position of delerict Tank will be reported at once to Battalion Headquarters.

9. **CONTACT AEROPLANES.** Contact Aeroplanes will fly over the ob--jectives at Zero plus one hour, at Zero plus two hours 30 minutes and Zero plus 4 hours and when ordered. Red Flares will be lit at these hours but Companies will not light them unless called for by Klaxton Horn or by the dropping of white lights.

10. **REPORTS.** Early information is of utmost importance and, in addition to reports, when the situation demands them, Companies will report at least every hour after Zero. Reports are required regarding:-

     (a) Progress of Attack.
     (b) Action of enemy.
     (c) Enemy movement.
     (d) Enemy strength.
     (e) Disposition of Enemy.
     (f) Reports on roads, bridges, rivers, crossings &c
     (g) Any destruction done by enemy to hinder our
           advance.

11 SIGNAL COMMUNICATIONS.

Instructions as to methods of communication will be issued .

12. PRISONERS.

Prisoners will be taken in batches direct to GOURNIER FARM where they will be taken over by Officer in Charge of Prisoners' Escort, who will give receipts. Escorts will not exceed 1 man to 10 prisoners and will be returned to Brigade Headquarters, – All papers will be taken from Officers and handed over by Escort with prisoners.

13. INTELLIGENCE.

Moppers up will search all German Corpses. German Identity Disc is divided into two parts and is easily broken. One half of disc and all papers will be collected and forwarded to Brigade Headquarters. Dugouts and shellholes will be searched and all documents sent to Brigade Headquarters.

14. SYNCHRONISATION.

Companies will send one Officer with at least two watches to Battalion Headquarters at 2 p.m. and 8.30 p.m. on Y day to synchronise watches with Battalion Intelligence Officer.

15. MAPS TO BE CARRIED.

No documents, maps showing other trenches, secret maps or papers (including private letters) will be taken into action, with the following exceptions:-
     (a) POELCAPPELLE Edition 3. 1/10000.
     (b) Map A.
     (c) Pigeon Message Maps (if provided)
     (d) Aeroplane Photographs.
     (e) Company, Platoon and Section Rolls.
     (f) A. B. 64.
     (G) REPORT MAPS

Acknowledge.

Capt. & Adjt.
9th Royal Scots.

Ya 32.

31 Rs.

CONFIDENTIAL

WAR DIARY

9ᵗʰ Battalion (Highlanders) The Royal Scots

From 1·10·17

To 31·10·17

Ref: roughly Lens Sh. 1/100,000
France Sh. 51B SW 1/20,000
57/B SW. 1/10,000
VISER Actions

WAR DIARY
or
INTELLIGENCE SUMMARY.

(Erase heading not required.)

Instructions regarding War Diaries and Intelligence
Summaries are contained in F. S. Regs. Part II.
and the Staff Manual respectively. Title pages
will be prepared in manuscript.

Place	Date	Hour	Summary of Events and Information	Remarks and references to Appendices
COURCELLES	1-10-17 to 4-10-17		The Battalion thus was again in billets in COURCELLES	S.L.
LINE	5-10-17		The Battalion left COURCELLES at 9.30 a.m. by bus and detrained at CRUCIFIX in STD, and marched to the line in front of WANCOURT in relief of 5/32, D.L.I. and 1 Coy 4th E. YORKS. The front held by the Battalion ⊕ extended from about O 26 A 75.90 to about O 20 B 13 – "A" Coy were in the right in the right "C" in the right "A" Coy in support and "B" Coy in reserve. "B" HQ were in BUCH RESERVE (about O 19 & B.1) – 4th Seaforth HQ were on the left and 153rd Inf. Bde on the right, the front was very quiet. Lunsford and Mac drummond provinces M 23 A 8.4	S.L.
– do –	6-10-17 to 8	10.30 a.m.	The line continued very quiet and marched at 10.30 a.m. to the line, arrived and meeting the trench were occupied by "C" and "D" coys, the support trench were occupied and about trench and "A" and "B" coys "A" and "B" Coys relieved by "C" and "D" coys respectively and carried on the work left off by A and B.	O.O.O.
– do –	9-10-17 to			O.O.O.
– do –	11-10-19		On night of 11th/12th a German raiding party was driven off by german [signature]	O.O.O.

A5834 Wt. W.4973 M687 750,000 8/16 D. D. & L. Ltd. Forms/C.2118/13.

WAR DIARY   9TH B 39(7H.) Lt. Royal Scots.

or

INTELLIGENCE SUMMARY.

(Erase heading not required.)

Army Form C. 2118.

Instructions regarding War Diaries and Intelligence
Summaries are contained in F. S. Regs., Part II.
and the Staff Manual respectively.   Title pages
will be prepared in manuscript.

BJ MAOS LENS Vimy
France Sheet 37 & S.W. 1/20,000
Vis-en-Artois 51 B S.W2 1/5000

II

Place	Date	Hour	Summary of Events and Information	Remarks and references to Appendices
LINE	11-10-17		9/R4 P patrols having 3 dead Germans, in front of our trenches, our casualties were 1 O.R. killed and 2 O.R. wounded and 1 O.R. missing. One of our patrols going out from O post encountered a German patrol of 30 men, shots were exchanged and both patrols withdrew, our casualties were 1 O.R. killed. Steps showing position of strafe was trained toward n attacked.	H.Q.O.
— do —	12-10-17		On night of 12th/13th we again sent out patrols, partly to recover bodies of our men who were killed on night of 11th/12th, the patrol failed to find the body and nothing of interest happened. No enemy patrols being out.	H.Q.O.
— do —	13-10-17		At noon of 13th inst the Battalion were relieved by 4 & 18th GORDON Hrs. and marched back to rest trenches by in YORK LINES after having been 8 days in the trenches. Total Casualties Killed 3 O.R. wounded 6 during this tour of the line there was great patrolling activity shewn by both sides.	H.Q.O. & P.Q.

[signature]

Army Form C. 2118.

WAR DIARY

or

INTELLIGENCE SUMMARY.

(Erase heading not required.)

Reg. Rath. LENS YPRES
FRANCE. SHEET 57 S.W. 1/20,000
1/15 — EN=FR=TO:5/57 S.W.2 1/10,000

9th Bn. (Terr.) 2d Regd/West.

Instructions regarding War Diaries and Intelligence
Summaries are contained in F. S. Regs. Part II.
and the Staff Manual respectively. Title pages
will be prepared in manuscript.

Place	Date	Hour	Summary of Events and Information	Remarks and references to Appendices
YORK LINES M22.b.8.3.	14-10-17		The battalion remained at YORK LINES and training was carried on at the camp was also improved (by detailed working parties.)	A.P.O.
— do —	15-10-17		The battalion carried on as on 14th in.	A.P.O.
— do —	16-10-17		Major General EDWARDS and staff (American Army) visited the battalion and inspected the physical Bayonet training, saluting. The work of one of the Coys. (D Coy)	A.P.O. A.P.O.
— do —	17-10-17 to 20-10-17		The battalion remained at YORK LINES and carried out training, working parties improved, Rifle, pathways and general improvement.	A.P.O. A.P.O.
— do —	21-10-17		The battalion relieved the 4th Bn GORDON Highlanders in the line 8 p.m. relief was completed by 12.30 p.m. The time in the line	A.P.O.
LINE Apex 5-10-17	21-10-17		rear of HAMECOURT. Patrol went out mighty but no enemy	A.P.O. A.P.O.
— do —	22-10-17 to		Patrol went out and no action took place Lewis Gun fire being directed on enemy working parties	A.P.O. A.P.O.
— do —	24-10-17		was very quiet shelling light directed on batteries in ... beyond	A.P.O.

A.5834 Wt. W.4973 M687 750,000 8/16 D. D. & L. Ltd. Forms/C.2118/13.

REF MAPS. LENS 1/10.000
FRANCE. SHEET 51 ª S.W. 1/20.000
5/ B.S. W? 1/40.000

Army Form C. 2118.

WAR DIARY
or
INTELLIGENCE SUMMARY.

(Erase heading not required.)

9th Bn (Tors) The Royal Fus (Regt)

Instructions regarding War Diaries and Intelligence
Summaries are contained in F. S. Regs., Part II.
and the Staff Manual respectively. Title pages
will be prepared in manuscript.

Place	Date	Hour	Summary of Events and Information	Remarks and references to Appendices
LINE	24-10-17 to		On 24th inst B & A Coys (support & Reserve) relieved C & D Coys in front line. no casualties were reported during the relief.	A.R.O.
— do —	28-10-17		The enemy became more active using GRANATENWERFERS on our posts, and shelling the left front Company. (5) shifting Signalling by lamp was reported and enemy barrages were observed by our Signallers, and decoded by Major THORBURN. The battalion was relieved by 2nd Bn. DUKE OF WELLINGTONS Regt. and moved by Motor bus to IZEL-LE-HAMEAU where it went into billets. Casualties for the tour of the line was KILLED 3 O.R. WOUNDED 4 O.R.	A.R.O.
IZELLE-HAMEAU	29-10-17 to		Training was carried on on training area round the village. The weather was very changeable.	A.R.O.
— do —	30-10-17		Draft of 1 officer (2Lt. R M. MURRAY) and 51 O.R. joined for duty.	A.R.O.
— do —	31-10-17		The Battalion remained at IZEL-LE-HAMEAU.	A.R.O.

[signature]

A5834 Wt. W4973 M687 750,000 8/16 D. D. & L. Ltd. Forms/C.2118/13.

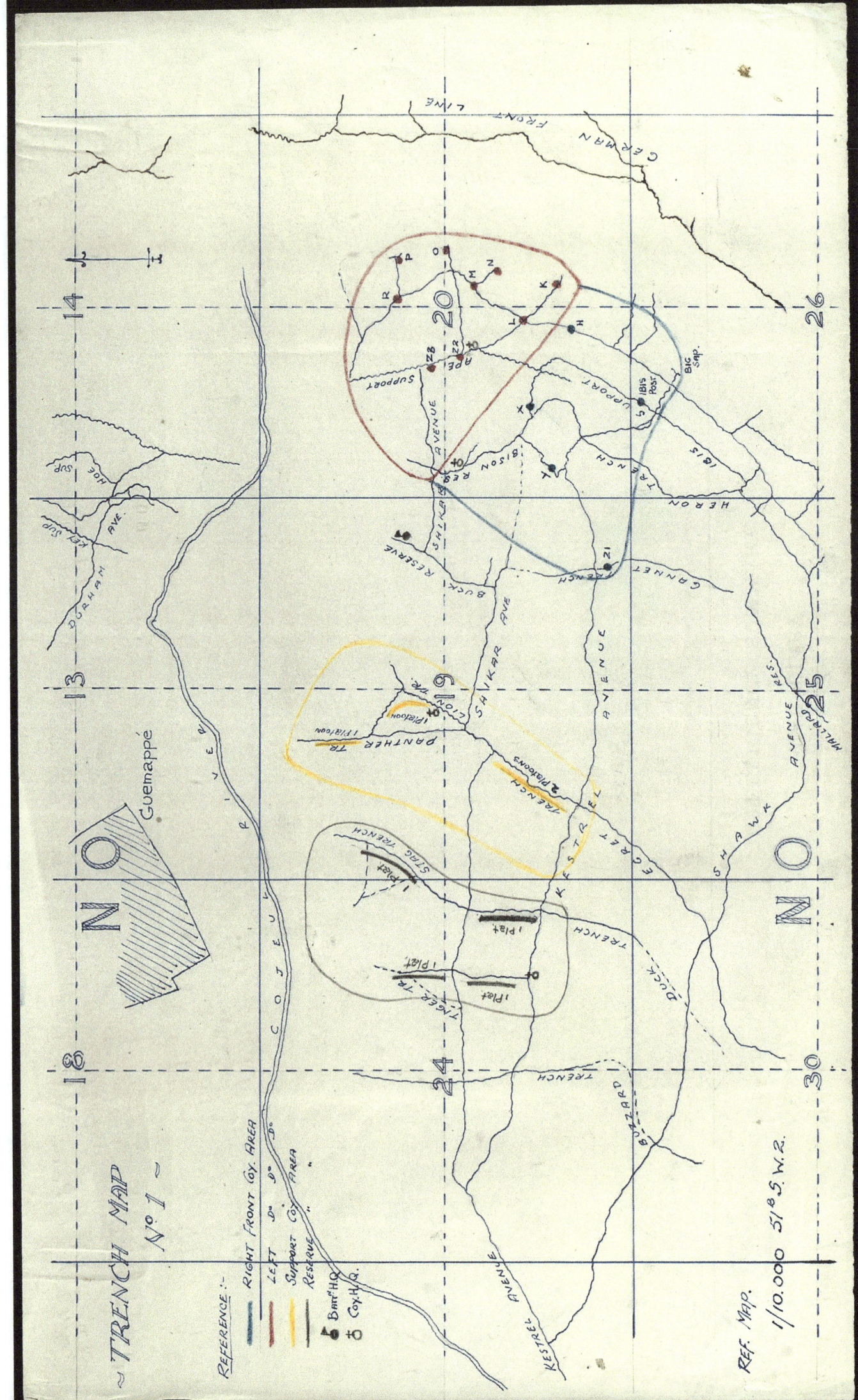

154th Brigade.

51st Division.

9th BATTALION

THE ROYAL SCOTS

NOVEMBER 1917.

Appendices :-

By Major LENS ¾₀.₀₀₀ HIERNIES ¹/₂₀,₀₀₀   9th Bn (Terr.) The Royal Fusiliers   Army Form C. 2118.

FRANCE 57ᴱ ¹/₄₀,₀₀₀
FRANCE 57·7·5·E. ¹/₂₀,₀₀₀
MOEUVRES 5ᴱ ¹/₁₀,₀₀₀

WAR DIARY
or
INTELLIGENCE SUMMARY.

(Erase heading not required.)

Instructions regarding War Diaries and Intelligence Summaries are contained in F. S. Regs., Part II. and the Staff Manual respectively. Title pages will be prepared in manuscript.

Place	Date	Hour	Summary of Events and Information	Remarks and references to Appendices
IZEL LEZ HAMEAU	1·11·17 TO 13·11·17		The battalion remained in billets and carried out training.	By P.S.
			The training arranged this day on a Holiday to celebrate the first Anniversary of the Battalion of ("BEAUMONT HAMEL. Brigade sports were held near "NOYELLE VION, and extra rations were issued for the occasion. Training was carried on in open tactics were practised by the battalion.	By P.S.
do —	14·16·11·17 15·11·17			By P.S.
— do —	16·11·17		The transport moved to [ ] MOYENNEVILLE Billets.	By P.S.
— do —	17·11·17		The battalion and battalion remained in billets.	By P.S.
			The battalion, (Her Echelon B. under command of LT R. M. SCOTT) marched to BEAUMETZ-LES-LOGES remained at IZEL-LEZ-HAMEAU) starting at 12.45 p.m. and entrained from there in BAPAUME arriving at 8.30 p.m. when the transport joined the battalion, having remained MOYENNEVILLE that morning.	
Bapaume 18·11·17			The battalion remained in billets in BAPAUME, till 5 p.m. when they proceeded via BAPAUME - LE TRANSLOY - ROCQUIGNY - BUS where the night was spent.	Hr P.S.
LEEHELLE 19·11·17 METZ 20·11·17			At 10.15 p.m. the battalion marched to METZ arriving at 12 m.n. on 20 L. LEEHELLE The battalion moved to position of assembly Q20b. at Q30am preparatory to attack on enemy defences. 1544 Inf. Bde. being in reserve. The battalion returned to METZ	Hr P.S. Hr P.S.
LINE 21·11·17.			At 3·30 a.m. the battalion moved to position of assembly (map Liberty) at 3·30 Front Line moving by route A- Q20.L.3.C.- Q22.L.1.9.- Q16 and to (See Reference Map attached)	By Q.S. By Q.S.

Instructions regarding War Diaries and Intelligence
Summaries are contained in F. S. Regs., Part II.
and the Staff Manual respectively. Title pages
will be prepared in manuscript.

WAR DIARY
or
INTELLIGENCE SUMMARY.

(Erase heading not required.)

Place	Date	Hour	Summary of Events and Information	Remarks and references to Appendices
LINE	24/11/17		Arrived in Old British front line at 6.15 a.m. and at 6.30 a.m. moved forward to HINDENBURG SUPPORT line. At 9.25 a.m. moved to Railway in K.24.d. On arrival at Railway at about 10.15 a.m. the Battalion moved forward in two lines of Companys N.T. 200 yards interval and 200 yards distance. Left Company directed and moved by eastern end of FLESQUIERES and east of ORIVAL WOOD. On reaching a line F.L.7.d.6.5. – L.8 central – Battalion was halted – Battalion Head quarters being established at L.14.a.0.6. and Close hast with a view to ascertaining developement of situation. At about 12.30 p.m. there appeared to be a large eastward movement. About L.8.b.9.1. One Company was seen to push forward to ridge from L.8.b.6.3. to L.8.b.4.3. to ensure this flank. At 1.25 p.m. orders were received that Battalion would be held in Brigade Reserve and companies were concentrated under cover at gun positions L.14.a.0.6. At 4.20 p.m. orders were received to relieve 4th Bn GORDON HrS. who were holding the line in front of CANTAING VILLAGE and east of CANTAING VILLAGE. Company Commanders at my request proceeded to reconnoitre, after battalion Commanders in companies had led fixed in conjunction with O.C. 4th GORDON HIGHS. Companies followed and the relief was complete by 3.45 p.m. O.C. 4th GORDON HIGHRS. All four companies were in front line while HQ. Coy considered W.P.S. in posts. One company 4th GORDON HIGHRS was held in reserve at about L.3.c.7.1.	W.P.S.

Army Form C. 2118.

Ref. Map. LENS 1/10,000. MEUVRES 5F/20,000.
FRANCE 57C 1/40,000
FRANCE 57C S.E. 1/20,000

9th 15th (Highrs) The Royal Scots

WAR DIARY
or
INTELLIGENCE SUMMARY
(Erase heading not required.)

Instructions regarding War Diaries and Intelligence Summaries are contained in F. S. Regs., Part II. and the Staff Manual respectively. Title pages will be prepared in manuscript.

MEURGNIES.
1/20,000

III

Place	Date	Hour	Summary of Events and Information	Remarks and references to Appendices
LINE	21-11-17		A squadron of QUEEN'S BAYS were in front line and two squadrons were in support. N.W. of CANTAING. 6 Vickers Machine Guns belonging to 9th Cavalry Brigade M.G.C. were deployed in front line and in support. 4 Vickers guns from 154th M.G. Company were also available. The front line extended from F.27 b.5.5. m. The left through F.28 a.7.3. – F.28 b.5.0. – F.28 a.4.5. – L 4 in touch and L.10.b. C.0.6. with the 152nd Report Right on left and BEDFORD REGIMENT on right.	D.O.S.
LINE	22-11-17		At dawn on 22nd S.C. right front company finding that L had got a good field of fire (owing forward the right to L.10.d.4.7. (SUNKEN ROAD) and consolidated trench ports. The BEDFORD REGIMENT conforming on his right and lining up with guns at this point. The left company moved forward to F.22 c.1.1. then line running from the point along road to F.28.a.7.3. At 9 p.m. a heavy counter attack was directed on FONTAINE and succeeded in driving out troops from the villages. 4th SEAFORTH HIGHRS then taking up a position making left of 9th ROYAL SCOTS and running N.W. through F.21 Central. The GERMANS advanced to road running through F.22 a.b. and at when they reached the point left Company opened heavy fire with rifles and Lewis Guns which stopped them front with	

A7092. Wt. W1128 9/M1893 750,000. 1/17. D. D & L. Ltd. Forms/C2118/14.

Instructions regarding War Diaries and Intelligence Summaries are contained in F. S. Regs., Part II. and the Staff Manual respectively. Title pages will be prepared in manuscript.

Ref. Rufs. LENS WOOD FRANCE 57135'/2500
FRANCE 57c'/4500 MŒUVRES 5th/4500

9th Br (Sco) KO Royal Rifles Army Form C. 2118.

WAR DIARY
or
INTELLIGENCE SUMMARY.
(*Erase heading not required.*)

IV

Place	Date	Hour	Summary of Events and Information	Remarks and references to Appendices
LINE	22/11/17		Advance and forced the enemy back to dead ground behind the road. Enemy attempted on five more occasions to advance to the line of this road, but were unable to face the fire and withdrew. This then commenced digging behind the ridge running from F22a and e. to wood A23 a and b. Left Centre Company attempted movement in wood F23 e and F29 a and b. Special thrusts of fire from Lewis guns at intervals. They were also able to co-operate with left Company firing on enemy attempting to advance in F22 d. The Cavalry have withdrawn in the evening which caused a ready intimated of Company boundaries during the night 22/23rd the Provisional Boundary being been altered the front line L.4.c.9.9. from the ridge BEDFORD REST. The right Company was withdrawn to reserve in L.3.c.9.9. the night Company necessitated a further readjustment of the three front Companies. During night (22/23rd) patrols were sent out from all companies but were unable to locate position of enemy. The Left Company exploited its front along SUNKEN ROAD F22.c.1.2. 50ft Bank built behind relieving 4th SEAFORTH HGHRS and 7th A. & S. H. Others left flank resting and remaining of F21.d.9.5. with	

F7092. Wt. W128 9/M12593. 750,000. 1/17. D. D. & L. Ltd. Forms/C2-18/14.

Army Form C. 2118.

Ref Sheet LENS 1/10,000 HIÉRENIES 1/20,000
FRANCE 57C 57SE 1/40,000   9th Bn (Tr.) The Royal Scots.
FRANCE 57C 57SE 1/20,000
MŒUVRES 57 1/20,000

WAR DIARY
OR
INTELLIGENCE SUMMARY.
(Erase heading not required.)

Instructions regarding War Diaries and Intelligence
Summaries are contained in F.S. Regs., Part II.
and the Staff Manual respectively. Title pages
will be prepared in manuscript.

Place	Date	Hour	Summary of Events and Information	Remarks and references to Appendices
LINE	23-11-17		At dawn touch was obtained with 4th Bn BLACK WATCH at F.21 Central and left drawn back accordingly. At 10.30 A.m. 152nd BRIGADE attacked FONTAINE. They apparently failed to reach the village and dug in in Battalion left and at F.21.a.0.2. In touch with left company 9th Sgt still lying at F.21.d.9.8. At about 12 noon touch over the frontage held by left platoon of 9th Bn ROYAL SCOTS. The boundary being F.22.c.1.2. the afternoon considerable enemy movement was observed between edge of wood F.23.c.0.5. and FONTAINE. Parti's of Fifth Company inflicted severe casualties on enemy by rifle and Lewis gun fire firing the afternoon wood in F.23.E. and F.29.a. was subjected to artillery fire at intervals. Lewis guns from left on fire Company co operating with batch of fire enemy movement having been observed there. Through out the period in front line every artilling was active. The Post all along the line lengthened to fire varying intervals at frequent intervals. Several casualties were inflicted. Total Casualties for tour ? 4 July. KILLED O.R. 4 WOUNDED O.R. 16. The battalion was relieved on night 23/24th by 2nd Bn GRENADIER GUARDS and marched back to billets in METZ &c. P.S.	V

9th 82 (4th) Tk Royal Scots   Army Form C. 2118.

WAR DIARY
or
INTELLIGENCE SUMMARY.
(Erase heading not required.)

VI

Instructions regarding War Diaries and Intelligence Summaries are contained in F. S. Regs., Part II. and the Staff Manual respectively. Title pages will be prepared in manuscript.

Place	Date	Hour	Summary of Events and Information	Remarks and references to Appendices
METZ	24-11-17		The battalion marched to YTRES arriving at 9.20 p.m. and entrained there for VILLE arriving at 9.30 A.M. on 25th where the battalion went into billets.	W.P.S.
VILLE	25-11-17 To 29-11-17		The battalion remained in billets and training was carried on, weather being changeable.	W.P.S.
—	30-11-17		At 2.30 p.m. the battalion received urgent orders to move to Roequigny and entrained at EDGE HILL STATION (BUIRE) at 5.30 p.m. for BAPAUME detraining at BAPAUME at 10.45 p.m. Marched via BEAULENCOURT - LE TRANSLOY to ROEQUIGNY arriving at 2.10 A.M. on 1st December the battalion went into Camp. The transport which had moved by road from VILLE to ROEQUIGNY joined the battalion i.e. The weather for these few days was good, and the health of the troops excellent.	W.P.S.

[signature]

Battalion

Report on

Operations

F.615.

TO

HEADQUARTERS

154TH. INFANTRY BRIGADE:

Reference Maps:- NIERGNIES,1/20,000 and France
57 C.S.E.,1/20,000.

Report on Operations on 20th.21st.22nd.and 23rd.
November:-

20th.November,1917:-

At Zero on 20th.November,9th.Royal Scots were
in billets in METZ.
They moved to position of assembly in Q.20.b.
at 9.50 a.m.
At 3.30 p.m. the Battalion moved back to
billets previously occupied in METZ and remained
in readiness to move at short notice.

21st.November:-

At 3.30 a.m. moved off to position of assembly
in old British Front Line moving by route "A" -
Q.20.b.3.6. - Q.22.a.1.9. - Q.16.d. and b . -
Q.11.Central.
Arrived in old British Front Line at 6.15 a.m.
and at 6.30 moved forward to HINDENBURG Support
Line.
At 9.25 a.m. moved to Railway in K.24.d.
On arrival at Railway about 10.15, Battalion
moved forward in two lines of Companies at 200
Yards interval and 200 Yards distance.
The left Company directed and moved by eastern
end of FLESQUIERES and East of ORIVAL WOOD.
On reaching a line L.7.d.6.5. - L.8.Central -
Battalion was halted - Battalion Headquarters
being established at L.11.a.6.0. and stood fast
with a view to ascertaining development of
situation.   At about 12.30 a.m., there appeared
to be a backward movement about L.8.b.9.1.   One
Company was sent to ridge from L.8.b.6.3. to L.8.
b.4.5. to secure this flank.   It was not required
and was afterwards withdrawn.
At 1.25 p.m. orders were received that
Battalion would be held in Brigade Reserve and
Companies were concentrated under cover at gun
positions L.11.a.6.0.
At 4.20 p.m. orders were received to relieve
4th.Bn.Gordon Highrs. who were holding the line in
front of Eastern end of CANTAING VILLAGE.
Company Commanders at once went forward to
reconnoitre after boundaries for Companies had
been fixed in conjunction with O.C.4th.Gordon
Highrs.   Companies followed and the relief was
complete by 3.45 a.m.
All four Companies were in front line
which was consolidated in posts.   One Company of
4th.Gordon Highrs. was held in reserve about
L.3.c.7.1.
A squadron of Queen's Bays was in front
line and two squadrons were in support N.W.of
CANTAING.   6 Vickers Machine Guns belonging
to 9th.Cavalry Brigade M.G.C. were disposed in
front line and in support.
4 Vickers Guns from 154th.Company were
also available.
The front line extended from F.27.b.5.5.
on the left through F.28.a.7.3. - F.28.b.5.0. -
F.28.d.4.5. - L.4.Central and L.10.b.0.3. -
Battalion was in touch with 4th.Bn.Seaforth
Highrs. on left and Bedford Regiment on right.

At dawn on 22nd., O.C. Right Company finding that he had not a good field of fire, swung forward his right to L.10.d.4.7. (Sunken Road) and con::structed fresh posts: the Bedford Regiment conforming on his right and touching up with him at this point.

The left Company moved forward to F.22.c.1.1. their line running from this point along road to F.28.a.7.3.

At 9 a.m. a heavy counter attack was directed on FONTAINE and succeeded in driving our Troops from the village. 4th. Seaforth Highrs. then taking up a position touching left of 9th. Royal Scots and running N.W. through F.21. Central.

The Germans advanced to road running through F.22.a.b. and d.; when they reached this point left Company opened a heavy rifle and Lewis Gun fire which stopped the advance and forced enemy back to dead ground behind the road.

Enemy attempted on five more occasions to advance to the line of this road but were unable to face the fire and withdrew. They then commenced digging behind the ridge running from F.22.a. & c. to wood A.23.a. and b.

Left centre Company observed movement in wood F.23.c. and F.29.a. and opened bursts of fire from Lewis Guns at intervals. They were also able to co-operate with left Company firing on enemy attempting to advance in F.22.d.

The cavalry were withdrawn in the evening which caused a readjustment of Company boundaries.

During the night 22/23rd. the Divisional boundary having been altered, the Bedford Regiment took over the front line to L.4.c.9.9. from the right Company. The right Company was withdrawn to reserve in L.3.c.9.9. This necessitated a further readjustment of the three front Companies.

During night of 22/23rd., Patrols were sent out from all Companies but were unable to locate position of enemy.

The left Company extended its front along Sunken road F.22.c.1.2. to get in touch with Unit relieving 4th. Seaforth Highrs. and 7th. A.& S.H. their left flank reaching and remaining at F.21.d.9.8.

At dawn 23-11-17, touch was obtained with 7th. Bn. Black Watch at F.21. Central and left drawn back accordingly.

At 10.30 a.m. 152nd. Brigade attacked FONTAINE.

They apparently failed to reach the village and dug in on Battalion's left and F.21.a.0.2. in touch with left Company, its left still being at F.21.d.9.8.

The right of 152nd. Brigade about 12 Noon took over the frontage held by left platoon of 9th. Royal Scots, the boundary being F.22.c.1.2.

Throughout the afternoon, considerable enemy movement was observed between edge of wood F.23.c. 0.5. and FONTAINE. Posts of left Company inflicted severe casualties on enemy by rifle and Lewis Gun fire.

During the afternoon wood in F.23.c. and F.29. a. was subjected to artillery fire at intervals - Lewis Guns from left centre Company co-operating with bursts of fire, enemy movement having been observed there.

Throughout the period in front line, enemy artillery was active, the posts all along the line being subjected to fire of varying intensity at frequent intervals. Very few casualties were inflicted.

The Battalion was relieved on night 23/24th.
by 2nd.Bn.Grenadier Guards and marched back to
METZ.

Machine Guns:-

The machine guns available in the Battalion
Sector varied in number,increasing during tour of
Battalion from 10 to 16.   They were disposed
in 3 Echelons:-
   (i) In vicinity of front line.
  (ii) As close support to front line on a line
       F.27.d.4.7. - L.4.a.4.4.
 (iii) Old German support trench L.3.b,c,d.
     The greater number were placed on North
side of CANTAING Road with a view to securing left
line.

Stokes Mortars:-

Six Stokes Mortars were used in vicinity of
F.28.Central to co-operate with artillery barrage
during attack by 152nd.Brigade on morning of 24th.
November,by firing on wood in F.23.c. and F.29.d.
Four were withdrawn on completion of duty and
two remained with Battalion until relief.

Ammunition Supply:-

Ammunition was brought up by pack.
A dump was formed by Battalion Headquarters
L.3.a.5.1. and a small forward dump at about
L.28.d.7.3. (also by pack).
About 64 Boxes in all were brought up.

Communication:-

Telephonic communication was maintained
practically the whole time with the three right
Companies.
There were a considerable number of intervals
during which wire was down to left Company.
Wire to Brigade was often down.
Runners were used to Companies.
Mounted orderlies were supplied for communic:
:ation to Brigade.
Only one message was sent by pigeon.

27th.November,1917:   Lieut. Colonel.
                Cmdg.9th.Bn.(Hrs) The Royal Scots.

Report on

Communications

9th Battn. (Highlanders) The Royal Scots

Report on Communication

During 22nd and 23rd November

During the night of the 21st and the morning
of the 22nd the Battalion moved up forward and
took over positions from the 4th Gordons who
were in communication with the 154 Brigade only.

At 2 am on the 22nd a line was run
forward through the village of Cantaing to the
Left Centre Coy. (A) to the Right Centre Coy. (D)
to the Right Coy. (C). A T-in was run to Left
Coy. (B). Communication was established with
all Coys. by 6.30 am.

A Direct Line was run from Battalion
Headquarters to the Right Coy. at 7.30 am

A Loop was run from outside Battalion
Headquarters round the left of Cantaing
to the line between Left and Left Centre Coys

On the 23rd the disposition of the
Coys was altered D Coy was now
Right Front Coy., A Coy Centre Front Coy
B Coy Left Front Coy, C Coy. in Support

A Direct Line was run to C Coy.
who had a T-in from the Direct Line
running to their old position. The
Line between C Coy and D Coy was
looped.

A Direct Line was run from
B Coy. to Battalion Headquarters.
A Line was run from A Coy to

B Coy. on the early morning of the 24th. The best route proved to be from Battn. H.Q. via D Coy to B Coy and loops were of great value.

Brigade Lines.

The Line to 154 Brigade H.Q. remained O.K. till 2 pm on the 22nd, from which time it was dis till 7 pm. The Line again went down about 10 am on the 23rd and was not "put through" as we were now working under the 152 Brigade to whose Headquarters (La Justice) a line was run by the 4th Gordons. This line was maintained by the Gordons and ourselves, a Test Station being established halfway. This station proved of great use.

On four occasions linemen went out on the line to the 152 Bde. H.Q and no breaks were found.

The 152 Brigade were very slow in answering when called, and information was thereby delayed.

Visual.

Communication by lamp was established with 154 Bde. H.Q. about 9 am on the 23rd. A priority message was received and two were sent before the lamp was destroyed by shell fire and the two operators became casualties.

Plans of communication are attached herewith.

Ref. Enemy Communication.

Lines at different parts were tested, but no signals were obtained.

Enemy cable, which was salved and afterwards relayed, was invaluable to us.

———

All lines to Coys. and 152 Bde. H.Q. were handed over to the relieving Battalion (2nd Grenadier Guards) O.K.

———

Pigeons

Pigeons were released from Battn. H.Q. on 23rd and, on the Cavalry leaving our front, their birds were taken over by us. Four pigeons were handed over to the relieving Battalion.

27/11/17

A.C. Mitchell
Signalling Sergeant
9th Battn. (Highlanders) The Royal Scots

LINE DIAGRAM OF COMMUNICATIONS ON 23RD NOVR 1917.

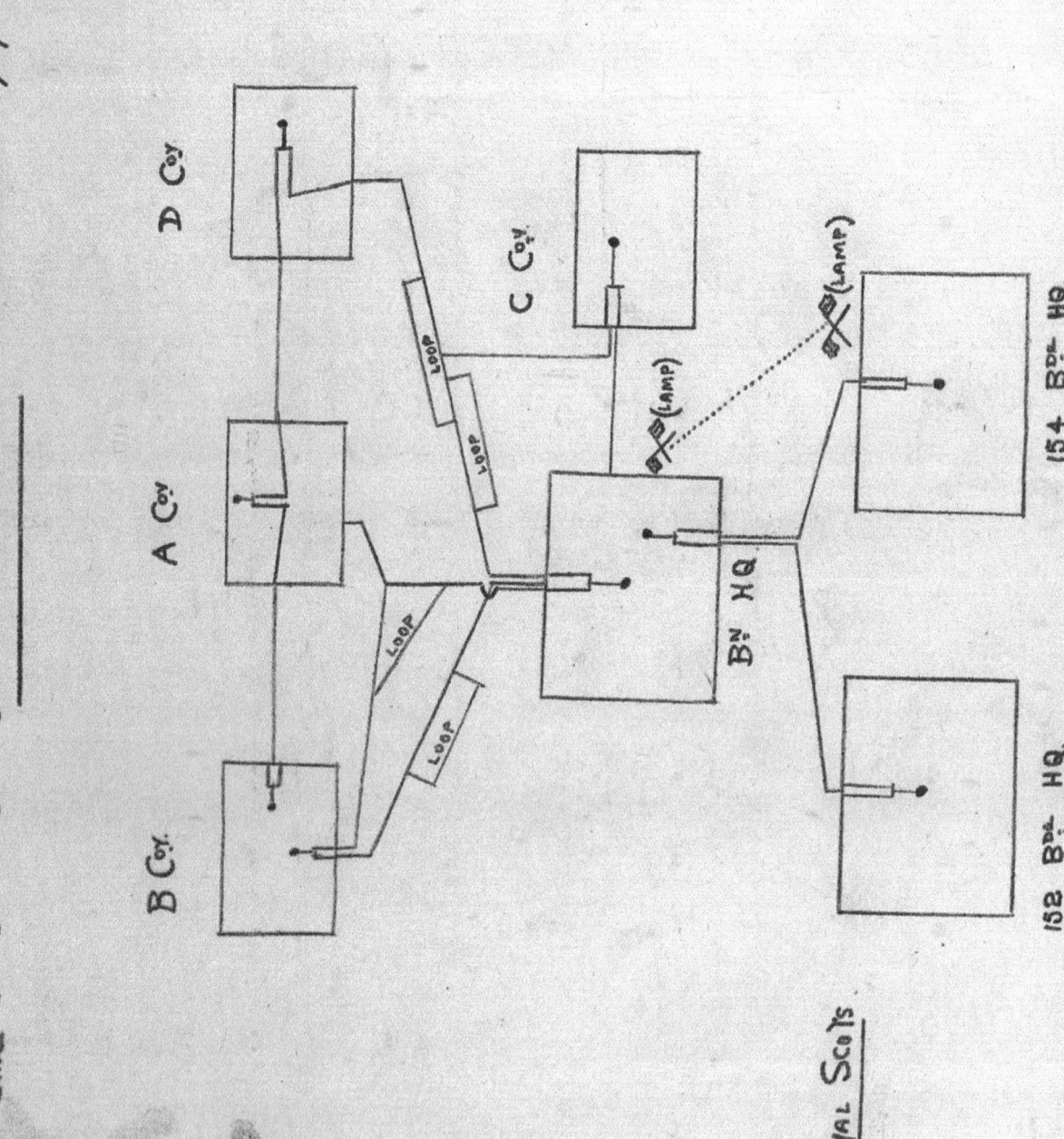

D COY.

C COY.

A COY.

B COY.

(LAMP)

(LAMP)

LOOP

LOOP

LOOP

LOOP

LOOP

BN HQ.

154 BDE. HQ.

152 BDE. HQ.

9TH BN. (HIGHRS) THE ROYAL SCOTS.

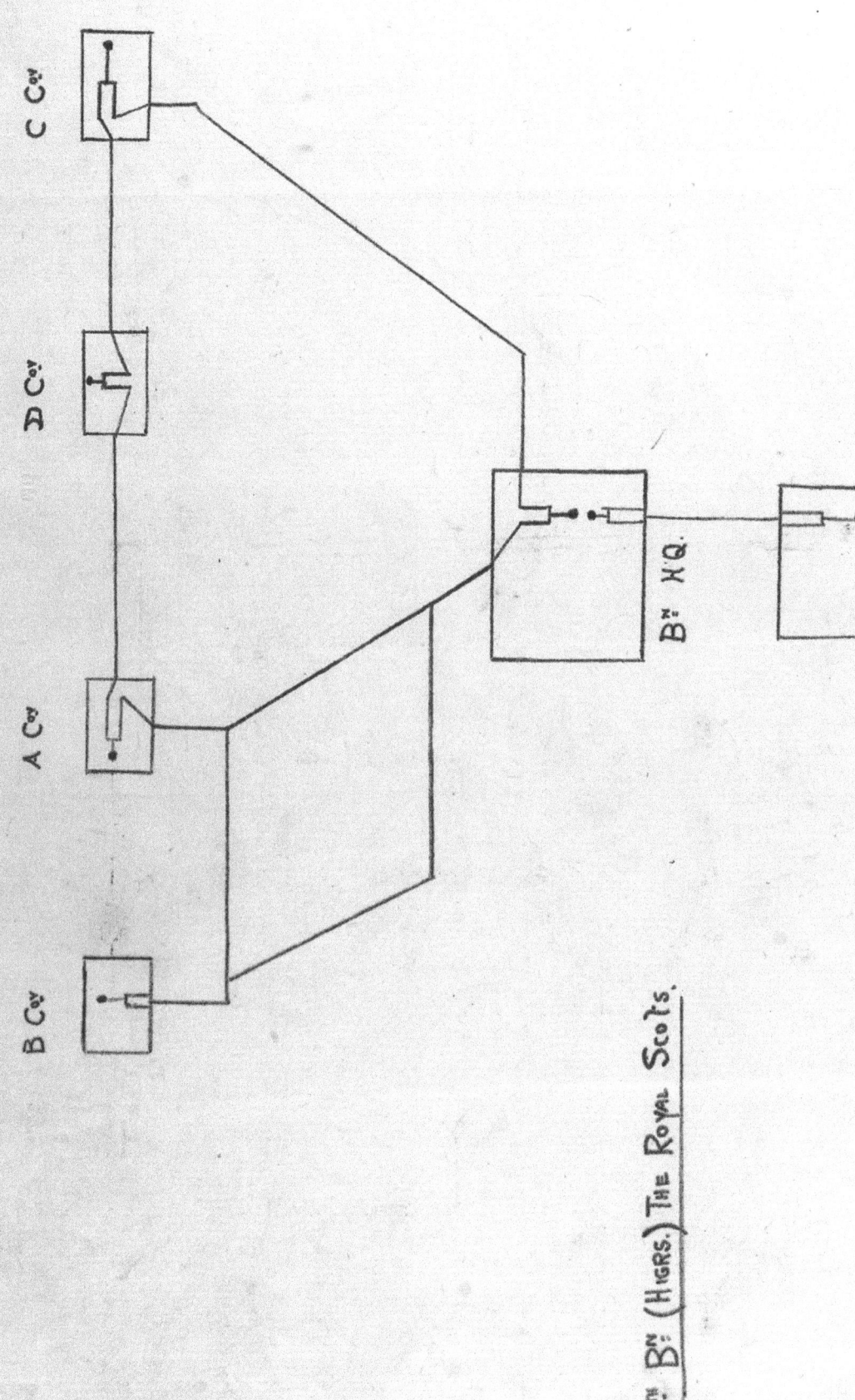

Line Diagram Of Bn Communications On 22nd Novr. 1917.

C Coy

D Coy

A Coy

B Coy

Bn HQ.

154 Bde HQ.

9th Bn (Higrs.) The Royal Scots.

BOUNDARIES: The 152nd. and 153rd.Inf.Brigades will make
good the semi prepared line NINE WOOD - BOURLON WOOD and
the villages of CONTAING.
From this point it is proposed to pass through
the 4th.Gordon Highrs. and 7th.A. & S.H. with the
objective FONTAINE NOTRE DAME, with outposts N. and E. of
Village.   9th.Royal Scots and 4th.Seaforth Highrs will
be in support.

INSTRUCTIONS FOR OFFENSIVE OPERATIONS A.1/2

Reference Map:

Sheet 57.C. 1/40,000

1. GENERAL.   On a date and at an hour to be notified later the
    Third Army will attack the enemy's lines from the Canal du
    Nord (just west of HAVRINCOURT) to the south on a two-Corps
    front.

    The object of the operation is to break the enemy's
    defensive system by a coup de main, with the assistance of
    Tanks; and to pass Cavalry through to gain further ground.

    The IV Corps will attack with 51st (H) Div. on right -
    62nd Div. on left - 6th. Division (III Corps) is on right of 51st
    (H) Division.

    51st (H) Div. attacks with 152 Inf.Bde. on right -
    153rd. Inf.Bde. on left.   154th.Inf.Bde. will be in Reserve.

2. OBJECTIVES AND BOUNDARIES: (1) Objectives and boundaries of Brigade
    and Battalions as in MARCOING Map issued to Companies.
        (2) First Objective: BLUE LINE
             Second Objective: BROWN LINE
        (3) Special instructions as to role of 154th.Inf.Bde. will
             be issued later.

3. ASSEMBLY: 9th.Royal Scots will assemble in METZ at Zero.

4. HEADQUARTERS: 154th.Inf.Bde - METZ
                   Battalion H.Q.- METZ

5. TANKS: a Battalion of Tanks will be employed on the front of each
            attacking Brigade.   The following signals will be
            employed for communication with Tanks:-
    All Clear, Come on,   " Red and Yellow Flag
    Tank broken down, dont -
                    wait.   " Shovel put through roof of tank.
    Tank wanted by Infantry - Helmet on rifle held above head.
        The above are the only prearranged signals between
    Infantry and Tanks.

6. ARTILLERY: The attack of the 51st (H) Division will be supported
    by two groups of Field Artillery.
        The whole essence of the operations being "surprise"
    there will be no preliminary bombardment. The attack
    will be made under a Field Artillery barrage to cover
    the advance of the Tanks.
        A percentage of guns will be used to form a smoke
    screen on the FLESQUIERES RIDGE, during the inital
    stages of the attack.

7. CONTACT AEROPLANES: Contact aeroplanes will fly over objectives
    at various times during Z day.
        Each Contact Aeroplane will be marked with a black
    rectangular disc 1½" x 1" on the rear edge of the lower
    plane on each side, and will fly along the line some three
    hundred yards in rear of our foremost posts, sounding a
    KLAXON HORN.
        The KLAXON HORN is the signal to get ready to light
    flares.   No flares will be lit till the airman fires
    a rocket or rockets.   Flares will be lit whenever called
    for as above, whether the time happens to be that ordered
    or not.

8. REPORTS: Early information is of utmost importance and in addition
             to reports, when the situation demands them, Companies
             will report at least every hour after leaving METZ. Reports

are required regarding:-

        (a) Progress of Attack
        (b) Action of enemy
        (c) Enemy Movement
        (d) Enemy Strength
        (e) Disposition of enemy
        (f) Report on roads, Bridges, rivers, crossings &c.
        (g) Any destruction done by enemy to hinder our
           advance.

9. SIGNAL COMMUNICATION: Instructions as to methods of communication
       will be issued.

10. PRISONERS: Prisoners will be taken in batches direct to
       TRESCAULT (Q.10.a.4.4) where they will be taken over by
       Officer in-charge of Prisoners' Escort, who will give receipts
       Escorts will not exceed one man to 10 prisoners and will be
       returned to rigade H.Q.   All papers will be taken from
       Officers and handed by escort with prisoners. Only weapons
       will be removed from N.C.Os and men.

11. MAPS TO Be CARRIED: In order to avoid any chance of information
       falling into the hands of the enemy, no documents, maps
       showing our trenches, secret maps or papers (including
       private letters) will be taken into action, with the
       following exceptions:-

ACKNOWLEDGE.   Capt & A/Adjt.
                                      9th. Royal Scots.

TO INSTRUCTIONS FOR OFFENSIVE OPERATIONS A.1/2:

COMMUNICATION:

Runners: 4 Runners per Company will go with Battalion Headquarters.

Signal Offices: Signal Offices will be as follows:-

Divisional H.Q.   - P.26.Central
Adv.Div.Exchange   - (Q.14.a.2.2)
Div.R.A.,H.Q.   - P.26.Central
Adv.Div.Arty. Exchange - (Q.14.a.2.2)
152 Bde.H.Q.- Q.10.d.3.6.
153 Bde.H.Q.-Q.10.a.5.4.
154 Bde.H.Q. - METZ

Communication between above will be by buried cable, supplemented by overhead and trench lines.

Visual: A Central Visual Station manned by the Divisional Signal Company will be established at Q.5.c.5.4.   Attempt will be made by the 152nd.Inf.Bde. forward party to pick up this station from the valley between K.36 and K.18.   Forward of the GRAND RAVINE as far as the FLESQUIERES RIDGE all the ground is visible at this station.

Pigeons: 2 Pigeons will be allotted to each Company.   A map is printed on back of pigeon message form.   This map will be carried to Corps Headquarters, written parts of messages only being telegraphed to addresses.   Map references must therefore be given as well as marking positions on Map.   Messages will be addressed to Battalion Headquarters.

Rockets: 2 Signal Rockets will be issued to each Company and 2 per Battalion Headquarters.   The range of these rockets is 1200 Yards.

Cipher: On Z day and until operations cease, messages by Power Buzzer will be sent in clear. After Zero, until further orders the D.3 telephone may be used.

S.O.S.   Rifle Grenades bursting into 2 RED and 2 WHITE.   In an emergency 2 RED and 2 WHITE very lights may be used.

Cavalry Corps S.C.S. 1" Green Very Light

ACKNOWLEDGE:

Capt & A/Adjt.
9th.Royal Scots.

Copy No. 1 to O.C. A Coy   Copy No. 6 to Medical Officer
"   " 2 " O.C. B "   "   " 7 " Signalling Sergeant
"   " 3 " O.C. C "   "   " 8 " Adjutant
"   " 4 " O.C. D "   "   " 9 " File
"   " 5 " Q.M.   "   " 10 " War Diary

Vol 34

War Diary

for

December 1917

of

9th Royal Scots

REF. MAPS FRANCE 57°N.W. Ed 7 B. 1/20,000
MEURVES 1/20,000

9th Bn (Co) Nile Royal (Rca)> Army Form C. 2118.

WAR DIARY
or
INTELLIGENCE SUMMARY.
(Erase heading not required.)

Instructions regarding War Diaries and Intelligence
Summaries are contained in F. S. Regs. Part II.
and the Staff Manual respectively. Title pages
will be prepared in manuscript.

Place	Date	Hour	Summary of Events and Information	Remarks and references to Appendices
ROQUIGNY.	1-12-17.		The battalion remained at Roquigny till 10 a.m. when it moved to BERTINCOURT	
BERTINCOURT			arriving at 11.35 a.m. where battalion went into billets. Battn. Hqrs. were warned and battalion was placed under orders to move at half an hour's notice. At 3.20 p.m. battalion (less Echelon "B" under command of CAPTN H. WAKELIN) proceeded to BEUGNY. On route counter orders were received and the battalion (less Echelon B and Transport) entrained at 5.30 p.m. at cross roads I.22. a.3.9. for the line. On arrival at J.9.b.8.2. the battalion detrained and guide of 2ND LONDON RIFLE BDE and met	
LINE			who conducted battalion to the line. The front taken over was between points- J.6. d.3.3. and K.7.d.3.5. and K.7.d.3.5. A Coy on right C Coy left centre B. Coy night ends and D Coy on ½ ½ Relief [2ND].L.R.B. being completed at 10.30 p.m. Line war, quiet and situation normal.	W.P.S.
LINE	2-12-17		At 4 p.m. the battalion (less B. Coy.) took over FRONT LINE from 1st L.R.B. between points E.19.b.1.1. and E.25.c.0.6. A and D Coys occupying FRONT LINE and C Coy support line between points E.19.a.4.2. and E.25.b.64. Battalion H.Q. being at E.25.b.2.4. Relief being reported complete by 9.40 a.m. B. Coy moved into position vacated by A Coy at J.6.d.3.3. Battalion remained as on night of 2ND DECEMBER till 5 p.m. when the battalion front was extended and B. Coy moved up from J.6.d.3.3. and took over front line from E.20.c.0.6. & E.20.c.6.3.	W.P.S.
LINE	3-12-17		INFANTRY between points E.20.c.0.6. & E.20.c.6.3. A bombing attack by the enemy being in progress the relief was not completed till 1 a.m. on the 4th inst. by this time the attack had been driven off and the line was quiet. During the day the 2ND HIGHLAND LIGHT during the day the battalion "B" marched from BERTINCOURT to the trenchport line at	

(A706) Wt W25 9/117293 750,000 11/17 D D & L. Ltd. Forms/C2118/74.

Instructions regarding War Diaries and Intelligence
Summaries are contained in F. S. Regs., Part II.
and the Staff Manual respectively. Title pages
will be prepared in manuscript.

WAR DIARY
or
INTELLIGENCE SUMMARY.
(Erase heading not required.)

Army Form C. 2118.

REF. MAPS FRANCE 57ᵉ N.W.Eᵈᵃ 1B ¹/₄₀₀₀₀
MŒUVRES ¹/₂₀,₀₀₀

4th. B (Sth) Lᵗʰ Royal Regᵗˢ
Ⅱ

Place	Date	Hour	Summary of Events and Information	Remarks and references to Appendices
LINE	3-12-17			W.P.S.
	4-12-17		I.28.a.&.2.	

At 4-45 a.m. 1 Company 4th. A.r.S.H. was attacked tactically to the Battalion
and took up a position behind B. Coy. between points E.25.b.6.4.
to E.24.c.1.1. At 4.20 a.m. the enemy attempted to bomb down the
gap in A. Coy. front at point E.19.&.3.0. but were repulsed, Raiding
sustained at least two casualties, and leaving a rifle in
our hands. At 3-35 p.m. the enemy made a second attempt
to bomb into our front-line on this occasion to
bomb down gap in E.28-&-8.th. B.Company front, and
fighting with bombs and rifle Grenades took place till
4-15 p.m. by which time we had inflicted several casualties
on the enemy and maintained our position. At 5-30 p.m.
orders were received that the positions held by the Battalion
were to be evacuated. A rear-guard of 1 platoon from each
of A.B.&C Coys. and two Creations were left in position till
4. a.m. n 5-th inst. by this time the remainder of the
Battalion had moved back to the rear of the British
front-line, which was being held at J.6.d.3.9. The
Battalion marched back to Camp in FREMICOURT and
by 8-30 a.m. the Battalion involving rearguard had reported
in Billets. Casualties for the tour of the line being KILLED 5 or WOUNDED 18 or.

| LINE | 5-12-17 | | | N.P.S. |

9th Bn (Ath) Yt Royal Scots

WAR DIARY
or
INTELLIGENCE SUMMARY.
(Erase heading not required.)

Instructions regarding War Diaries and Intelligence Summaries are contained in F. S. Regs. Part II. and the Staff Manual respectively. Title pages will be prepared in manuscript.

Place	Date	Hour	Summary of Events and Information	Remarks and references to Appendices
FREMICOURT	5-12-17		The battalion spent the afternoon cleaning clothing and equipment.	W.P.S.
	6-12-17 TO 9-12-17		Training was carried on and the battalion remained in billets, weather being very cold and dull. Improvements made to camp.	W.P.S.
	10-12-17		As the battalion was mostly employed on fatigue training was practically informal.	W.P.S.
	13-12-17		A draft of 4 O.R.s joined for duty.	
	14-12-17		Working parties were discontinued and the normal training was resumed.	W.P.S.
	15-12-17		A draft of 9 O.R.s joined for duty.	
	16-12-17		The battalion remained at FREMICOURT, training was carried on, Lt J.W. UNDERWOOD, 2d Lt F. FINDLAY and 2d Lt T.C. JACKSON joined for duty. The battalion left FREMICOURT at 4-30 p.m. to relieve the 14th GORDON H⁷³. in the line NORTH of BOURSIES. A Company was on the right, B Coy in the Centre & C Coy on the left, D Coy being in reserve in and around the village of LOUVERVAL. The night J.6 a. 7.3 m. the night to D.29 a.6.h. Batt. H.Q. being at D.28.d. & O. The relief being reported complete by 12.20 a.m. on 17th inst.	G.P.S.
LINE	17+2-17		Very quietly weather a slight fall of snow and very cold, front very quiet.	G.P.S.
do	18-12-17		On the morning of the 18th the battalion took over from the 4th Bedford H⁴⁵	G.P.S.

A7092- W: 128 9/M1293 75000 1/17. D.D & L. Ltd. Forms/C2718/14.

WAR DIARY

or

INTELLIGENCE SUMMARY

(Erase heading not required.)

Instructions regarding War Diaries and Intelligence Summaries are contained in F.S. Regs., Part II and the Staff Manual respectively. Title pages will be prepared in manuscript.

Place	Date	Hour	Summary of Events and Information	Remarks and references to Appendices
LINE 18-12-17			An additional part of the line and handed over a part to the 7th A+S.H. on the right of this battalion. New battalion boundaries being from J.6.a.3.3 to D.29.a.3.?.	
do	19-12-17 TO 20-12-17		Companies being the same as on the 16th inst reading from right to left. The battalion front was still quiet and weather quiet, working parties repaired the trenches, digging, saps, clearing communicating trenches and making improvements generally, endeavouring to write up front.	
do	22-12-17		The battalion was relieved by the 6th Seaforth Hrs. the relief being completed by 6-30 p.m. and marched back to camp in FREMICOURT. Rain places in the battalion lead subjected from 8th to 18th DEC at 35 P. During the last two enemy patrols were very active but no enemy patrols were met. NO MANS LAND. Casualties were KILLED 3 O.R.	
FREMICOURT. 23-12-17			WOUNDED 11 O.R. The battalion remained in camp and clearing of clothing and equipment was carried out, weather fine and cold. At 5-30 p.m. an enemy air raid commenced and bombs fell in the vicinity of the battalion area. One dropped in the camp and caused casualties.	

WAR DIARY

or

INTELLIGENCE SUMMARY.

(Erase heading not required.)

Instructions regarding War Diaries and Intelligence Summaries are contained in F. S. Regs., Part II. and the Staff Manual respectively. Title pages will be prepared in manuscript.

Place	Date	Hour	Summary of Events and Information	Remarks and references to Appendices
FAMECOURT	23-12-17		KILLED 2 O.R. Wounded 1 Officer (2Lt W. PATON) 4 O.R. The Enemy Shelled for an hour and a half 5-30 pm till 7 o'clock.	
do	24-12-17		An Aeroplane of ours raided on the 23rd 9 Lewis Gun for Anti-Aircraft defence - two Wounded and manned from Coys till Daylight.	
do	25-12-17 (CHRISTMAS DAY)		A General Holiday was observed and extra rations issued to the men. A Coy Show at the Division Cinema Show being arranged. Weather very hard a thaw early in day gave way late on to sleet and later on.	
do	26-12-17		Various Coy competitions ordered by the B.G.C. were cancelled owing to heavy fall of snow which took place during the forenoon.	By J.K.B.
do	27-12-17		Weather unusual cold and frosty, work was carried on in camp constructing trenches for practice against E.A.	By J.K.B.
do	28-12-17		Weather unusual cold work in connection with the camp trenches was continued, in the forenoon a Brigade shooting competition took place in which No 2 & 3 sections of 5 Platoon were runners up and "winners up" respectively.	By J.K.B.
do	29-12-17		Weather still cold frosty work in connection with above trenches was continued 2 Lt the Cannon 9th R.S. joined for duty.	By J.K.B.

A7092   W¹ W1128 9/M/293 750,000. 1/17.   D. D. & L. Ltd.   Forms/C2118/14

REF MAPS— MOEUVRES 1/20.000

Army Form C. 2118.

9th Bn. (Sco.) The Royal Scots

WAR DIARY

or

INTELLIGENCE SUMMARY.

(Erase heading not required.)

VI

Instructions regarding War Diaries and Intelligence
Summaries are contained in F. S. Regs., Part II.
and the Staff Manual respectively. Title pages
will be prepared in manuscript.

Place	Date	Hour	Summary of Events and Information	Remarks and references to Appendices
FREMICOURT	30th 12-17		The Battalion left FREMICOURT AT 12 noon to relieve the 8th A. & S.H. in the line east of DEMICOURT. D Coy in the front line and C in support. A & B Coys being in reserve at LEBUCQUIERE. Bn front was from K7a 8.2 to K.8 & 8.5. Bn Headquarters at K.7. d. 2.0. Relief was reported complete by 4 pm.	Appx 13. Appx 8.
LINE	31— 12-17		Hand front prevailed, front quiet. Casualties 1 O.R. (wounded)	

[signature] Lieut. Major
Comdg. 9th Royal Scots.

A7092. W: W128 9/M1/93. 750.000. 1/17. D.D. & L., Ltd. Forms/C2118/14.

Confidential

—

War Diary

—

9th Battn. (H.Q.) The Royal Scots

—

From .. 1st Jany 1918.

To 31st Jany 1918.

Ref Maps - France. 57° N.W. ED. 4B 1/20,000.
Moeuvres. ED. 5° 1/20,000.

WAR DIARY
or
INTELLIGENCE SUMMARY.
(Erase heading not required.)

9th Batt. (H's) The Royal Scots. Army Form C. 2118.

Instructions regarding War Diaries and Intelligence Summaries are contained in F. S. Regs., Part II. and the Staff Manual respectively. Title pages will be prepared in manuscript.

Place	Date	Hour	Summary of Events and Information	Remarks and references to Appendices
LINE	1/1/18.		D. Coy. in the front line. C Coy in support and A.B. Coys. in reserve at LEBUCQUIERE. Our front was from K.7.a.8.2. to K.8.a.8.5. Battn H.Q. at K.7.a.2.0. The line was quiet. Working parties engaged during and in the construction of dugouts and cubby-holes in the front line. Weather very cold and hard front.	J.S.
LINE	2/1/18.		Line quiet. Large working parties were up from Reserve Coys. on night of 2nd/3rd. Patrol was out our front but no enemy seen. Weather thaw. Slight thaw.	J.S.
LINE	3/1/18.		During the forenoon the line was quiet. Enemy aeroplane was forced to land at E.27.C.2.6. about 11 a.m. Inter-Company relief took place. D Coy relieved C Coy. A Coy relieved C. Coy. Relief complete by 6.30 p.m. At 4-4.25 p.m. the relief was delayed on account of heavy artillery fire going on to the right of our front. Gas shells were reported on our right, but no gas was reported in our sector. By 6.15 p.m. the situation quiet. 2/Lt. J.D.B. Leslie joined for Duty.	J.S.
LINE	4/1/18.		Situation was quiet. Our aircraft was active during the afternoon. Working parties engaged in Dug out shafts. Weather cold. Hard front. Patrol of 1 Officer and 8 o.r. was out along our front but no enemy encountered. Observation was good and much enemy movement seen.	J.S.
LINE	5/1/18.		Hard front. Line quiet. Ground haze hindered observation. Our aircraft was active patrolling behind our front line. Work continued in Dug out shafts.	J.S.
LINE	6/1/18.		Hard front till 4 p.m. then freal. Rain at 8 p.m. Trial barrage put down one and a half minutes after signal had been given. Work continued in Dug out shafts and cubby holes. Line quiet. Our aircraft actively patrolled our lines all day.	J.S.
LINE	7/1/18.		Fresh and very wet until mid-day. Work continued in Dug outs. Observation bad owing to haze the Battalion was relieved in the line by the 8th A. & S.H. Relief reported complete by 4-4.25 p.m. Battalion proceeded to MIDDLESEX CAMP. FREMICOURT. Situation quiet. During Platoon moved left in to line to be relieved by moving.	J.S.
FREMICOURT	8/1/18.		Party of 1 O.O.R. and 2 officers engaged working on wire at the BEAUMETZ-VAULX line under R.E.'s commenced at 9-30 a.m. Remainder of Battalion remained in camp cleaning clothing, equipment etc. Hard front and snow. Draft of 9 O.Rs. joined for Duty.	

Add. Maps.: FRANCE 5-7⅛ N.W. FB. 18. ~~20,000.~~ 20,000.
MOEUVRES. ED. 6⅛ ~~20,000.~~ 20,000.
LENS 11. ~~100,000~~ 100,000.

9th Batt. (Rifles.) 2nd Royal Scots.   Army Form C. 2118.

WAR DIARY
or
INTELLIGENCE SUMMARY.

(Erase heading not required.)

Instructions regarding War Diaries and Intelligence Summaries are contained in F. S. Regs., Part II. and the Staff Manual respectively. Title pages will be prepared in manuscript.

Place	Date	Hour	Summary of Events and Information	Remarks and references to Appendices
FREMICOURT.	9/1/18.		Battalion remained in Camp. Hard frost. Snow in the afternoon. During the day men were principally engaged in fatigue work, and digging practise.	
FREMICOURT.	10/1/18.		Weather fresh and cold. Battalion remained in Camp. A working party of 350. O.R. and 7 officers were up working near DOIGNES making a trench for cable. Casualties:- 1 O.R. killed. 1 O.R. wounded.	
FREMICOURT	11/1/18		Draft of 108 & 4 O.R. arrived. Weather fresh and slight rain. "Batt." parade at 12 noon for C.O.'s inspection and presentation of congratulation cards from G.O.C. Division.	
FREMICOURT	12/1/18.		Weather fresh and cold. Working party of 350. O.R. supplied. Battalion engaged in digging drains and laying floorboards round huts.	
Do.	13/1/18		Battalion stayed in MIDDLESEX CAMP. Weather changed, sleet and snow.	
Do.	14/1/18			
Do.	13/1/18.		At 1.30 p.m. the battalion marched to LEBUCQUIERE.	
LEBUCQUIERE	18/1/18 TO 19/1/18		4th SEAFORTH. HRS., the battalion was in Brigade Reserve, weather very wet and a high wind blowing.	
Do.	18/1/18		Battalion remained in billets weather very wet and cold.	
Do.	19/1/18		The battalion was relieved by 2nd Batt. D.L.I. and marched off at 1.40 p.m. to COURCELLES -LE-COMTE via FREMICOURT, BAPAUME. ACHIET-LE-GRAND. arriving at 6.15 P.M.	
COURCELLES -LE-COMTE	21/1/18		Battalion left COURCELLES-LE-COMTE at 9.10 a.m. and marched via. AYETTE, ADINFER, TRANSART, to BAILLEULVAL, arriving at 1.35 p.m. Battalion went into rest billets.	
BAILLEULVAL	21/1/18.		Battalion spent day cleaning up, and repairing billets.	
Do.	22/1/18		Training was commenced on ground in vicinity of billets, weather mild and wet.	
Do.	30/1/18 TO 31/1/18.		Battalion remained in billets. Training was carried out. Weather dry and inclined to be frosty. Battalion inspection and presentation of ribbons by Gen. S. M. Harper K.C.B. D.S.O. commanding division. Detached men of T.M.B. and M.G. Coy returned to duty. Numbers who joined for duty during the month 2/Lt. S.D.M. LESLIE. 2/Lt. F.B. MOFFAT (ret.) from 954 T.M.B.) O.R. 78.	
Do.			The weather for JANUARY has been cold but dry and the health of the troops very good.	

J.?.?.L. Comm. 9 Royal Scots

A3792. Wt. W108 9/M4f23 250,000. 1/17. D. D.& L. Ltd. Forms/C2-18/11

9th Battn (Hrs) The Royal Scots   Copy Nº 8

OPERATION ORDER Nº 141

Reference Maps
57ᴄ 1/40,000
MOEUVRES 1/20,000

1 RELIEF   The Battn will be relieved by 8th
                A. & S. Hrs on 9th January and on
                completion of relief will proceed
                to MIDDLESEX CAMP, FREMICOURT

2. GUIDES   Guides will be provided as per attached
                table. They will be furnished with
                slips showing post or platoon which
                they represent.

3 TRENCH STORE The following will be handed over:—
  & WORK   (a) All Trench stores, Maps, Defence
                    Schemes. etc
                (B) Details of work on hand and
                    proposed

4. STORES   Socks, salvage, water tins, mess
                stores & cooking utensils of Coys
                in the line will be taken to Bn Ration
                Dump before 3 p.m. One man per
                Coy will be left in charge & one
                nco to be detailed by O.C. B Coy.

5. **LEWIS GUNS** — Lewis Guns of A & B Coys will be taken to Ration Dump after relief. 1 NCO per Coy will be left in charge until arrival of transport

6. **MINING PLATOONS** — Mining Platoons will be relieved at work at 12 noon on 8th January. Shifts will return to camp independently on completing last task

7. **TRENCH STORE LISTS** — Lists of trench stores handed over will be forwarded to O. Room by 10 AM on 8th Inst.

8. **COMPLETION OF RELIEF** — Completion of relief will be reported by code word "FREEZING"

9. **RESERVE COYS** — C & D Coys will move to MIDDLESEX CAMP on the morning of 7th January. OC C Coy will arrange with OC 8th A.S.H. as to time camp will be vacant Coys must be clear of LE BUCQUIERE by 2.30 pm

10. **REAR COYS ADVANCE PARTY** — OC C Coy will detail an advance party of 1 officer & 8 OR to take over MIDDLESEX CAMP at 9 AM on 7th January

11. A.A. LEWIS   Same Lewis Gun anti-aircraft posts
    GUN POSTS   will be taken over in MIDDLE-
                SEX CAMP and manned by
                C & D Coys until arrival of
                remainder of Battalion.

12. ECHELON "B"   Echelon "B" will rejoin the Battn
                  in MIDDLESEX CAMP at 4 pm
                  on 7th January

13. TRANSPORT   Necessary transport for LEWIS
                Guns & Stores of front line Coys
                will be at Battn Ration Dump at 5.30 pm

14.   Arrival in camp will be
      reported to O Room.

15.   ACKNOWLEDGE

                        Jas Stevenson
                             Lt Col Adjt
Issued at 4 pm.
 6-1-18   9th Royal Scots
  DISTRIBUTION
  Copy no 1 O.C. A Coy   Copy no 6   T.O.
        2   " B "   "   7   Q.M
        3   " C "   "   8   C.O ✓
        4   " D "   "   9   Adjt
        5 O.C. Ed "B"   "   10   Z.M
                               "   11   O.C 8 " & 8A

RELIEF TABLE

	GUIDES	TIME & PLACE
A Coy	1 per HQ	Entrance to TROUT ALLEY
	1 per Platoon	K 7 c 3.6. — 3pm
B Coy	1 per HQ	
	1 per Post	do
C Coy	none	
D Coy	none	
Bn Hq	none	

Sequence of reliefs

B Coy   POSTS A. A'. X. B. C. D. E. F.
          Coy Hq. G. H. K.

A Coy   Platoon in WALSH SUPPORT, 1st Platoon
JAFFREY, Coy Hqrs, 2nd Platoon
JAFFREY, Platoon at Bn Hq.

OPERATION ORDER NO.143:

Copy No. B

14th January 1918.

Reference Map:
Sheet 57c.N.W.
1/30,000

1. **MOVE:** The 9th.Royal Scots will relieve the 4th.Bn.Seaforth Highrs in LEBUCQUIERE tomorrow 15th.inst.

2. **STARTING TIME:** 1.30 p.m.

3. **STARTING POINT:** Road opposite Orderly Room

4. **ROUTE:** Overland track to T.27.Central - FREMICOURT ROAD - LEBUCQUIERE. Road

5. **ORDER OF MARCH:** H.Q., A.B.C.D. 200 Yards between Companies.

6. **MINING PLATOONS:** Mining Platoons will be organised before leaving Camp and will march in rear of their Companies.

7. **ADVANCE PARTY:** Advance party of 1 N.C.O. and 1 man per Platoon and 1 N.C.O. and 1 man for Battalion H.Q. will parade behind Orderly Room at 9.30 a.m. on 15th.inst. under Lieut.T.D.H.LAWSON and will proceed to LEBUCQUIERE and take over accommodation from 4th.Seaforth Highrs.

8. **GUIDES:** Guides will meet the Battalion at entrance to LEBUCQUIERE.

9. **STORES:** All blankets and valises will be stacked behind Orderly Room by 10 a.m. All Mess Stores will be stacked behind Orderly Room by 1 p.m.

10. **LEWIS GUNS:** Lewis Guns will be loaded on Lewis Gun Limbers by 12 Noon

Capt & A/Adjt.
9th.Royal Scots.

ACKNOWLEDGE:

Issued at.......p.m.

Copy No.1 to O.C. A Coy   Copy No.8 to T.O.
"   " 2 " O.C. B "   "   " 9 " Q.M.
"   " 3 " O.C. C "   "   " 10 " M.O.
"   " 4 " O.C. D "   "   " 11 " Lieut.LAWSON.
"   " 5 " Specialist Officers "   " 12 " Adjutant
"   " 6 " O.C.4th.Seaforth Hrs."   " 13 " War Diary
"   " 7 " H.Q.154th.Inf.Bde. "   " 14 " File.

Reference Maps:
Sheet 57.C.1/40.000   OPERATION ORDER NO.143:
LENS 11 1/100.000   --------------------------

1.   MOVE.   The Battalion will be relieved by 2nd.Bn.D.L.I.
               tomorrow 19th.inst., about 12 Noon and on
               completion of relief will march to COURCELLES-
               LE-COMTE.

2.   STARTING TIME: About 12 Noon.

3.   STARTING POINT: Junction of Road and Railway -T.29.b.9.4.

4.   ROUTE: FRELICOURT - BAPAUME - AVESNES-LES-BAPAUME -
                    ACHIET-LE-GRAND, - COURCELLES-LE-COMTE.

5.   ORDER OF MARCH: H.Q.,B.C.D.A.   200 yards between
                         Battalions.   100 yards between Companies.
                         Pipers with their Companies.

6.   BLANKETS AND   Officers valises,,blankets, canteen and signalling
      STORES: stores will be stacked at Orderly Room by
                       6.30 a.m.   Mess Stores will be stacked at
                       Orderly Room by 12 Noon.

7.   ADVANCE PARTY: Lieut.H.SHIRLAW and 1 N.C.O. per Company will
                     take over accommodation at COURCELLES-LE-
                     COMTE, reporting to Staff Captain,134th.Inf.
                     Brigade at Town Major's Office, COURCELLES at
                     11.15 a.m. on 19th.

8.   DRESS: Full Marching Order - Steel Helmets strapped on
                packs - Leather jerkins will be worn.

9.   TRANSPORT: Cookers and Water Carts and Mess and Medical Carts
                    will move with the Battalion Remainder of
                    Transport under orders of B.T.O.

10.   DINNER: Dinner will be at 11.30 a.m.

       ACKNOWLEDGE :

                                              Capt & A/Adjt.
       Issued at.......p.m.   9th.Royal Scots.

       Copy No.1 to O.C. A Coy   Copy No.7 to M.O.
        "   " 2 " O.C. B "   "   " 8 " Specialist Officer
        "   " 3 " O.C. C "   "   " 9 " Lieut.H.SHIRLAW
        "   " 4 " O.C. D "   "   " 10 " Adjutant
        "   " 5 " Q.M.   "   " 11 " File
        "   " 6 " T.O.   "   " 12 " War Diary

OPERATION ORDER NO. 44.

Reference Map:
ISMS.11.A/18.000

1.   MOVE.   The Battalion will move to BAILLEULVAL tomorrow 20th.inst.

2. STARTING TIME: 9.10 a.m.

3. STARTING POINT: Road in front of Camp.

4. ORDER OF MARCH: HQ.,C,D,A,B, Companies and Transport. 200 yards between Battalions and 100 yards between Companies. Pipers with Companies.

5.   ROUTE: AYETTE - ADINFER - RANSART. Road North of BERLES AU BOIS - E. of BAILLEULMONT.

6. BLANKETS AND   Valises, Blankets and stores will be at Q.M.Stores
     STORES: by 8 a.m. Mess Stores at H.Q.Mess by 8.15 a.m.

7. ADVANCE PARTY: Lieut.H.SHIRLAW and 1 N.C.O. per Company will report to TOWN MAJOR, at BAILLEULVAL by 11 a.m. to be shown accommodation.

     NOTE:-   Companies and Transport will be on road ready to move off by 9.10 a.m.

     ACKNOWLEDGE:

Capt & A/Adjt.
9tn.Royal Scots.

Issued at........p.m.

19th.January,1918.

Copy	No.	1	to	O.C.	A Coy	Copy	No.	7.	to	M.O.
"	"	2	"	O.C.	B "	"	"	8.	"	Specialist Officers
"	"	3	"	O.C.	C "	"	"	9	"	Lieut.H.SHIRLAW
"	"	4	"	O.C.	D "	"	"	10	"	War Diary
"	"	5	"	Q.M.		"	"	11	"	Adjutant
"	"	6	"	T.O.		"	"	12	"	File.

Lightning Source UK Ltd.
Milton Keynes UK
UKOW07f1104130516

274165UK00006B/17/P